I0124205

Seasons in the Pine Barrens

Seasons in the Pine Barrens

The Journal of Miriam S. Moss

South Jersey Culture & History Center
2023

Published in 2023 by the South Jersey Culture & History Center
at Stockton University

South Jersey Culture & History Center
Stockton University
101 Vera King Farris Dr.
Galloway, New Jersey 08205

Title: Seasons in the Pine Barrens:
The Journal of Miriam S. Moss

Author: Miriam S. Moss

Copyright © 2023 Miriam S. Moss

Design copyright © South Jersey Culture & History Center

ISBN: 978-1-947889-15-6

All rights reserved. No part of this work may be reproduced or
transmitted in any form by any means, electronic or mechanical
including photocopying and recording or by any information
storage or retrieval system without permission in writing from
the author, except in the case of brief quotations embodied in
reviews and certain other non-commercial uses permitted by
copyright law.

The mission of the South Jersey Culture & History Center
at Stockton University is to help foster awareness of the
rich cultural and historical heritage of southern New Jersey,
to promote the study of this heritage, especially among
area students, and to produce publishable materials that
provide a lasting and deepened understanding of this heritage.

stockton.edu/sjchc

This book is dedicated to Sidney Moss

Welcome Reader

Time and nature flow through all of us. Although no one can fully capture these ineffable currents of life, I spent years observing and participating in the natural world in New Jersey's Pine Barrens and recording thoughts in my journal.

During that time, I was mostly in my 50s and 60s, married to Sidney. Our children were into their college years and beyond. For many a weekend, over almost thirty years, we two lived in our secluded primitive cabin.

Our cabin was a simple place, on 25 acres of land, next to the Greenwood Branch, a tributary of the Rancocas Creek. It was built in the 1920s of local wood by local persons, with a central fireplace, woodshed, and nearby outhouse. There was no electricity. The cabin had a gas refrigerator, a four-burner gas stove, and a hand pump in the sink provided water for boiling and washing.

This book represents my thoughts generated by quietly sitting in the cabin observing flora and fauna, and considering life and nature in the world of my time. The journal entries were written in ink for myself, and have been edited only for readability. I have grouped the entries here by season, with each entry dated. I often wrote when I sat on a rocking chair looking through the floor-to-ceiling screens facing the stream below, or when I sat at the living room table in the light of our two kerosene lamps. They still speak to my deepest feelings, now at age 92, much as they did when they were written decades ago. My hope is that these words will also be meaningful to you.

Author's Note

The photos in this book were all taken by me, across the seasons, over more than three decades. They are included to add a visual dimension for readers and as another way to share the experience of life in this special place.

They reflect my continuing interest in preserving Pine Barrens images, large and small, that I have enjoyed and treasured. None of these photos were taken in association with any of the written entries in my journal.

MSM

SPRING

Cabin in spring

March 15, 1996

Time and the Stream

As I look at the dark grey water with small ripples, an occasional bit of leaf or of foam floats downstream. The flow of the stream seems to be the passage of time. Water and minutes go by, passing but never to return.

I can understand the water. It comes into view far to my left, and swirls around the bend, leaving with silvery bands off to my right. The water began somewhere—in underground aquifers upstream. And it will go somewhere—out to the larger stream, to the river, and out through the Delaware Bay to the ocean. There are maps that tell me this. I have seen the water upstream and downstream.

But the undercurrent of time is much less clear, not understandable. Time is nothing I can touch, it's not wet or dry. Where does it come from? Go to? Or are these the wrong questions to ask?

I might theoretically be able to catch up with a small amount of water, but time? It's only captured as a reflection, a memory.

Fern arising

Fern Opening

March 18, 1989

Few Changes in Cabin

We have done so little to change things in and around our cabin over the past ten years. Last month we took a big step—and bought a wood stove so we can come here more comfortably overnight.

Also we have a new bird feeder filled with sunflower seeds. Often during the day there are processions of chickadees, titmice, and nuthatches, and, of course, several red squirrels stopping by to eat the dropped seeds.

The two changes have been a real pleasure. Yet I have a little guilt in adding to the simplicity of our place.

Down here I enjoy having little I must do: no bathroom to clean, no utility bills to pay. Just one yearly propane tank for the gas stove and the refrigerator. I do heat up the pot to get hot water. And I often remove a half dozen white-faced hornets from the screened windows.

I cherish the rhythm we've built into our daily lives down here. Although each day is different from others, we tend the garden, walk trails, cook and eat, read, listen to music, and now with the wood stove, Sid has found pleasure in chopping wood.

March 23, 1980

Bagworm

The sun was warm and it cast a branch's shadow across the outhouse wall. I stood by the weathered wooden outhouse—watching a caterpillar, closely examining its ways. I saw the bagworm close up the end of its sack. Maybe it will stay put for a few days—long enough to split off and shed its old, outgrown skin. I wondered about it. I was oblivious to the trees, the sky, the birds.

Usually when I look so closely at nature, I think about my life or our times, and see mirrored in the microcosm of the natural world, the patterns and problems of men. But today, this kind of analogy didn't come to mind—I felt open to it, but I didn't search for the parallel.

I am 50 years old. Most important to me today is *me*. I don't know where I want to go and be. Somehow being here—in the warm sun—watching and listening to spring signs is just right. But gnawing underneath is the uncertainty—of the world, and of what I want to do in it.

I know that I'm that bagworm—this place is my cocoon, and I am shedding my skin.

April 5, 1985

Away from the Push and Pull of Everyday Life

In *Moby Dick* there is, from the beginning to end—an inexorable drive, a movement at times pulling one (to sight the whale, to go out to combat the whale); at other times pushing one (Ishmael's desire to leave the land, the winds of the huge storm). Ahab was the drive personified. His direction was set; he knew and the reader knew where he was going. Maybe some of the profound appeal of the book, and of novels, plays, stories in general is this *direction*, this sense of movement, this plot.

Perhaps the appeal of plot is that our lives, in general, have unclear plots, vague directions, no explicit, inexorable drives. Rather, for much of our lives we focus on *being*, as we grow up from infancy to full size, find companionship, reproduce and nurture our kind, as we focus on learning and on work. I would guess that the unique multiple themes by which each of us live are intertwined, contradictory. The flow of our lives is more a web than the single strand of a clear plot.

Down here at the cabin, lying on the hammock, I'm listening to the whispers of the breezes and feeling the intermittent coolness wipe off the moist warmth on my bare arm. Here is where I feel I am *being*. Not directed outward, not pursuing some external goal, but here I feel solid, and here I am away from the push and pull.

I can doze, feel the hammock's response to the wisps of air. I can watch the pine branches brush the blue sky.

April 9, 1995

Easter Sunday

The sweet gum buds are swelling. The arbutus is mostly in tight buds. We had a very hard freeze in mid-week, reminding the bushes that warmer days will continue to be interrupted by frosts.

No phoebe has come this spring. Maybe they recall that last year their multiple efforts to nest yielded no young; maybe the controlled burning of near woods scared them off to less vulnerable spots; maybe their wintering places were inhospitable and they didn't survive.

No matter, the feeling of a spring without phoebes leaves a void. Each year I've wakened to their rhythmic call. I've watched the birds bring mud, grasses and twigs to their nest. I've tried to peek at the nest to see the miraculous eggs.

Maybe the birds will come later this spring. Their presence has little meaning to my work-a-day world, or to my life in my suburban home and garden. But the phoebe has a place in the pine woods here. What if early April came with no arbutus in bloom? There is a sequence of expected blooms and birds, of leaves coming out, and of leaves coloring before they fall. When this pattern isn't followed it is as if the rules of the seasons are broken. A sprig of arbutus' sweet blooms is on the table now. But the phoebe's call is missing.

April 29, 1995 NOTE: Phoebes began their nest last week—now it's finished with 4 eggs. The world seems right.

April 11, 1992

Two Mallards

Two mallards swam by upstream. Female led male as they came toward the curve of the slate grey water. A few circles of raindrops patterned the water around them. When we paddle our canoe upstream, we are quite insulated from the water. Even as we dip our paddles, we keep our fingers dry. It takes a decision on my part to feel the water—sometimes I don't put my hand in the water, sometimes I do.

The mallards are "in" the stream in a way I've never been. When I go into the water, it is to be refreshed on a hot day, or to feel the stream and swim against it for a few moments. But I am mostly a stranger to the creek.

Mallards seem to use the waterway much as I walk a trail. It's a place where I put one foot ahead of the other, look around, move from one place to another. When we are in the canoe, then are we on the stream much as the mallards are? Maybe so, but we miss the immediacy of the water—much as we are separate from the terrain when we drive in a car.

When I first noticed the mallards I was aware of their swimming against the current. And I wondered if they go up, as often as down? How far do they go upstream? Are they eating along the way? Seeking a nesting place? Just looking around?

April 12, 1985

Inside and Outside

The cabin is cozy, dry, the wood stove is hot, the kettle is boiling and calls for Sid's tea. The fireplace cradles logs wrapped in yellow flames tinged with strips of blue. We're comfortable inside.

We do go out many times during the day: to get wash water from the stream, to the garbage pit, to the outhouse. And when we're out we hear and see the pine barrens world. Listening brings sounds of the earliest whippoorwill, of flocks of geese, of familiar calls from unseen birds.

If we were to have modern conveniences here, we would go out less, hear less, see less, and focus on artificial clock time and calendar time. We would miss the rhythm of the woods, stream and sky.

I have brought a few sprigs of arbutus into the cabin to refresh us with its perfume and the beauty of the world outside.

Arbutus

April 15, 1989

Less is More

Why do I enjoy the vast differences between our home and the cabin? Most people with second homes have similar facilities in each—certainly running hot and cold water, central heating, inside toilets—and electricity.

This second, simpler world helps me to make a statement—lots of things are unnecessary, less is more, sparseness is fullness. We still sleep in a warm bed, have a good roof over our heads, and have refrigeration for our food. We have books to read, paper and pen for writing. The cobwebs get swept away from the chair rungs when I feel like it. The carpet sweeper takes care of the old braided rug.

Two upholstered chairs by the wood stove are comfortable. We can hear the rain as it drips from the roof and the trees, and maybe a crackle from the wood stove. Otherwise, the loudest sound is my pen writing on the paper.

April 15, 1989

The Water Pump

Shortly after Thanksgiving, we disconnected the pump to allow all the water to drain out to prevent it from freezing. During the winter months we use stream water for washing. Four buckets a day seem to be enough.

We set up the water pump today. Once again, we have the convenience of simply raising and lowering the pump handle and water runs right into the sink. It's not potable water, at least we don't drink it, or wash fruits/vegetables in it, not even use it for tea. The pump makes our lives a bit easier, and, in some way it adds to the complexity of our lives. Setting up the pump includes trial and error. After soaking the leathers, it's not easy to make a tight seal. After an hour of making adjustments, remembering how we did it in the past, it's done for another season.

At home we have instant water, hot and cold, in five, no six, sinks in the house, plus tubs and showers, and the outside faucets. It's nice here to have one simple pump. That's plenty high tech for me.

April 15, 1989

The Wood Stove

A wood stove is interesting. It's not simply a matter of setting up newspaper, kindling, and larger pieces of wood, then lighting a match. There's need to control the air intake so it starts to burn well, but later doesn't overheat. And today I learned that stoves burn better in cold weather. Then there's more draft, more suction of air up the chimney. On this warm, damp, calm spring day we can't get a good enough draft to close the damper and burn the wood cleanly.

April 20, 1985

Lamp Light

The temperature dropped this afternoon, so we have a fire going. Now, the room's all dark except for the circle that glows around the kerosene lamp on the dining table, and the flickering yellow flame that comes from the fireplace where the two logs meet.

Most of the room is in shadow, but the light is plenty bright on this journal. Everything an arms' reach away is lit up on the lamp's side. The ladderback of the chair casts a shadow more than six feet long. The small area of light keeps my focus close in.

When I'm home in town at night, the whole room is bright. The light can draw my attention away, distract me. Is there too much light in my world? Things that I'm not interested in are often as bright as things that I want to see.

Here, at night in the cabin, I can think about one thing at a time. There's no TV or phone. I'm quiet and writing.

Tea Berries

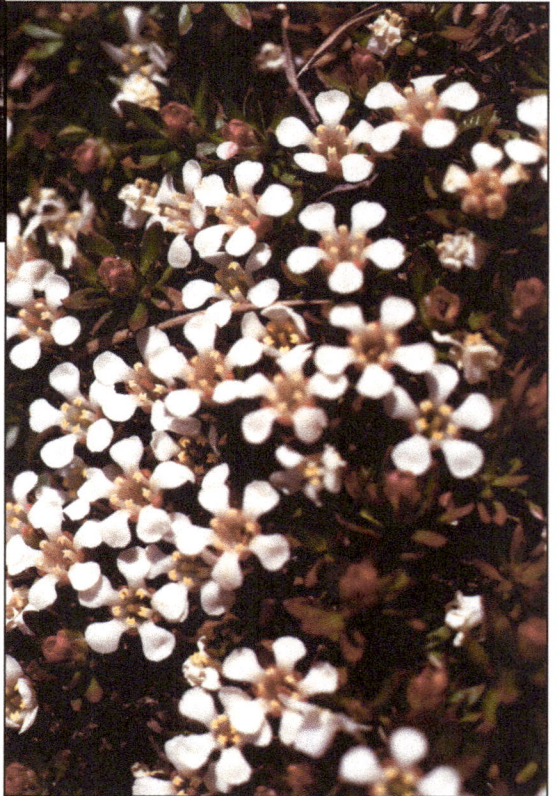

Pixie Moss

April 22, 2001

It's Spring Again

Once familiar bird songs are in the pines and oaks. Yellow birds, butterfly warblers fly, land on a branch long enough for me to spot them in my binoculars, but not quite long enough for me to carefully look for identifying colors, patterns.

Each spring I do remember the brown cap and the bobbing tail of the palm warbler; the "other" songs of the towhee; the pine warbler's trill. It's so often a new experience to watch and identify a bird, and an old experience, too. Each year there's a subtle addition. I know the white throat of the myrtle (yellow-rumped) warbler, but now I see how strong the black marks are on its chest.

I listen, and confuse memories with current sights and sounds. It's a process of remembering, relearning and seeing even more than in the past. I look at the bare branches in the woods near the stream. I see the white puffs of new shadbush blooms, and the swollen buds of more shadbush in the shade.

And each walk brings new delights, the arbutus in full bloom and its special perfume in the middle of the lane. I see the white peeking out of pixie moss buds.

This year's red fruit of the tea berries are so large, swollen with their subtle sweetness.

Spring brings the new, and lets me revisit the memories of past springs. What if each season came anew, not following patterns of the past?

Here at the cabin, spring is overlaid upon the winter past, with the summer and autumn to come.

April 24, 1994

Looking at the Stream

The late afternoon sun is full on me as I sit, looking through the screen. Three large pieces of wood have floated downstream and are stuck in bushes across the creek. A white-faced hornet is sunning inside the screen, motionless. I can look past it to the small sweet gum with green tufts of leaves from the ends of each branch, and then to the old laurel bushes with buds tightly closed, and on to the swamp maple at stream edge.

Towhees call. The male towhee rustles in the dry oak leaves. The wind tosses the branches. A pair of titmice and a pair of chickadees flutter in, each snatching a seed from the feeder. A white breasted nuthatch flits onto the feeder, takes a seed and leaves. Now a small red breasted nuthatch takes its place.

The sun is the whitest of white as it shimmers on the stream's surface.

April 25, 1999

Ticks

The prevalence of ticks and Lyme disease around here is well known. Right now, the hairs on my neck move ever so slightly signaling the presence of a tick. Two ticks had earlier crawled up my shirt. I dropped all three ticks into the little kerosene jar we keep nearby. Now I feel a tiny movement among the hairs on my shoulder. Sid looked, no tick there.

Here, we wear white clothes all the time: that is white underwear, shirts (usually long sleeve), pants (again full length), white polypropylene socks, canvas shoes. We spray with Deet, and we check ourselves and each other after being outside, even after going to the outhouse. We do a body check when we get up in the morning, and again when we get to our suburban home before we shower. We've taken the 3 shots against Lyme that are said to be effective immunization.

These ticks are also a protection for us. They discourage visitors from the city, so we have most time alone.

April 26, 1985

It is Spring

Arbutus are past their prime, though there are still quite a few fragrant white blooms in shady places. Sand myrtle blossoms, too, are mostly past.

The blooming plants are not early. This is their time to flower. Plants in the cooler, darker places where there's less moisture, bud later and bloom later. They are in perfect sync with their world, just as the earlier bloomers. Each responds to its inner-outer balance in its own way. Their timing is perfect.

I saw the first gypsy moth larva of this spring. Tiny thing, crawling across our brown and white plastic tablecloth. I crushed it with my finger, one less gypsy moth to eat our oaks later on.

April 28, 1989

The Now

I'll be 60 years old in September. In general, that means one more year beyond 59, not yet to that big number 65 that divides middle age from old age. I'm active, healthy and creative—not yet a grandmother.

There is a comfort and pleasantness in living in the now. Most all of our days at the cabin reflect a focus on the joys of now. We have few plans for the future here, except that the future will be much like today—the cabin warm and comfortable, the stream dark and cool, the pines and oaks dominant in the woods. Only the vegetable garden reflects our intrusion into the world of now and presents a potential of crops to eat, growing in enriched sandy soil.

Of course, we harbor the myth that our children will value this place, the cabin, its streams and woods. But know that its real value is for now, there is no saving up for the future. In 50 years (2039!) this could be a jewel, a rare retreat from a modern world I cannot imagine. But by then only our grandchildren could enjoy it, or great grandchildren.

As I look out and see two male towhees sparring over a small patch of stream-side shrubs, I expect that their descendants will continue to vie over territory in these woods, that they'll nest here—near the brown stream. Who knows how well-protected this land is from concrete culverts and housing developments.

For now, it seems to be an eternal place, similar to what it was 50 to 100 years ago, and similar to what it will be years from now.

I'm just passing through and can sit here, now, in the midst of it all, comforted by its eternal qualities.

Sheep Laurel

April 29, 1989

Rain

It's starting to rain. There are wet dots on the entry step, and a myriad of small, spreading circles on the stream. With few leaves now out, we have less tree cover than in later months, but even now there is a sense of shelter from the trees.

We welcome rain here. It means nourishment for our garden. We used to carry 10 to 20 buckets of water up to the garden each weekend, but in recent years we reserve our watering to the early days of seedlings and then leave the rest to nature. The results are the same. Our sandy soil is so porous, water quickly runs through it, and we just depend on rain.

Sid is back near the outhouse planting 6-inch cedar seedlings. No need to water them today. It takes ten years to get a fairly large tree. We are now very fond of the cedars and mountain laurel we put in when we moved here in 1979. We have a sense of kinship with these plants. Many laurels are now beginning to bear flowers. We've simply moved them, and scores of sand myrtle, from one place to another. They all belong here in the pine barrens, and they grow well.

May 2, 1992

Two Worlds

Do I live in two worlds? These quiet woods, where our reality is largely shaped by the changes in the seasons, the weather, the trees, birds, insects. And the other world shaped largely by other people—work, family, friends—all in the context of a complex society (rich and poor, white and non-white, young and old).

Here at the cabin we are quiet, letting only a little of the other world in through newspapers and an occasional news broadcast.

I can look over the darkening stream, at the patterned outline of tall pines and sweet gum trees in the distance.

Just before dark two canoes of noisy young men paddled by. They had passed an hour earlier going upstream and we decided they were "outsiders." Earlier in the afternoon Rick, neighbor downstream, with his dog paddled by. He belongs to this place, grew up here and feels it's part of him. He handles the canoe as a solo better than the two of us do together.

Is this an escape? A different world? Here, a regularity of whippoorwills' songs at dusk and dawn define our days. Our nearest neighbor, Jim, breaks our solitude by his infrequent visits. And on our strolls down the lane, if sometimes we do meet a neighbor, we'll chat for a few minutes about the weather and other stream-side residents.

At my workplace office there's a picture of the cabin. It's a reminder of this place, a different lifestyle, a quiet time in our lives when outside social demands are minimal.

And here in our cabin we do bring work to do—sometimes ignoring it for several days. At other times, focusing on it, and somehow blending our two worlds. I know they are not separate parts of me. They are interwoven. When I'm here I carry my *oughts* and *shoulds* from work, family, friends. When I'm home I feel reassured that a change in my life is awaiting me next weekend.

My world is one and complex. When I am here, I can pretend I am away from demands of myself and others, but I know I have only a hiatus, a temporary stepping out of a fast pace, into a gentle, quiet time. Here I do empty my mind and listen. I sit and look at a tree, at the stream, at an insect. Time goes by quickly here, and I sit quietly, to wait, to wonder.

May 4, 1985

Seasons

The male wren is singing softly, gently, near the nest box at dusk. Usually he sings with such vigor that his whole body makes the song vibrate. In a few minutes the whippoorwill will start to sing. If the evening weren't so cool, we could probably see bats flying over the stream. Unless the weather is very rainy or windy, these events occur every evening. That is the way things are.

People may be born, have worries, joys, and die, but the evening sounds of early May are repeated nightly, yearly. These sounds belong to no one. Others can enjoy them just as I do.

I wait, listening and watching the sky slowly dim. Now the whippoorwill begins, urgent, calling—briefly. It's right on time. Yet, there is a thrill when it happens. I'm reassured that things are in order.

This natural rhythm, rightness, year after year is comforting. So different from the world of politics, of our children, and from the work-a-day world. Here the weather may change, which is "natural," and the calendar may vary slightly each year, as the seasons follow each other.

May 5, 1984

Time Moves On

It's spring. The weather is warm enough today, everything seems to be moving along at the usual pace (warblers and "punkies," gypsy moths and oak leaves beginning)— everything, that is, but me.

The pace is very fast. I can't keep up with it. Perhaps that's a natural feeling at this time of year when we miss a regular weekend at the cabin. Two weeks is a long interval and much happens!

I notice more little changes each year, and I try to recognize each one as new and memorable. I look for, or am confronted by, many bird calls, buds, flowers, insects, many shifts from a long winter's dormancy to this incredible surging, burst of green spring.

Tonight, we knew from past journal entries, to listen for our first whippoorwill song of the season at 8:15 p.m. We were prepared for it. Yet the clear notes are a miracle. The annual cycle, no matter how regular and expected, sends a start through me. I catch my breath, my heartbeat quickens. It comes as a surprise, though it's right on time!

I know the wren will build her nest, the sand myrtle will bloom, the grey birch will grow another six inches, and each will occur regardless of what I do. I feel a tug from the woods and stream—to come on, keep up, to step in time.

May 10, 1992

Not Ready To Leave Yet

Sid is ready to pack up the car and drive home. But I'm not ready to leave yet.

There's a light, steady rain this morning. Raindrops make many circles on the stream. We moved the winter clothes upstairs today in anticipation of warm days to come. The floor guard in front of the wood stove has been wiped, ready for summer storage.

The leaves of most every bush and tree are growing—pale and delicate. Only the sumac and sour gum buds are still tightly closed. How much energy and power must be behind the unfolding of spring leafing out. Over a short few weeks the grey brown woods turn green.

I can accept this swift transition into spring. I feel its speedy pace and know I have no choice, no way to slow its greening. The timing of going home, leaving the cabin, *is* under my control.

I want to stay awhile—to listen to the phoebe and see if she nests nearby, watch the hummingbird as she returns sporadically to the feeder we put up just last evening, look again at the birdsfoot violets that will be on the wane next week. I want to see the patterns of new leaves, the tiny promise of pink in the laurel buds.

I know that next week these woods will have taken a giant step into spring. If I look carefully now, maybe I can be more sensitive to next week's changes.

Sid has emptied the refrigerator, taken the suitcase to the car, and is impatient to leave. I'm still not ready to leave.

Stream near cabin

May 15, 1987

Outside

I'm writing in my journal, looking out of the large screens with the double doors wide open. The afternoon sun is coming in.

Part of my attention is always alert to the woods and stream outside. The male wren has returned again and again to the nest box, singing a bubbly song on a nearby branch to lure the female. The large heavy-bodied carpenter bees are gliding by. An unknown bird calls insistently from the tall sweetgum across the stream. A lone black duck zooms over. A black and white warbler hangs upside down on a nearby branch, and then it finds a few insects on the pine that's leaning over the water.

The leaves on the sourgum seem larger than they were early this morning.

There's a quivering sound in the stream—a catbird bathing?

Raucous caws—and clunks—from a crow across the stream.

The phoebe calls incessantly. I don't know where she's nesting this year. I just went out to look, but saw no nest.

I notice, right next to the cabin, six pink buds from an azalea I'd never seen. Next to it, there is no sign of the climbing fern we had planted several years ago.

What a busy world this is! No people around. Except two men and a boy canoed down a few hours ago. One looked up at the cabin and remarked, "I bet that's a nice place inside." And here I sit, looking and listening . . . toward the outside.

May 15, 1976

Time

This and a few other entries were written in 1976–1978 when we rented neighboring cottages before we bought our cabin in 1979.

I don't wear a regular watch, but I do have a clock inside me. Nothing mysterious about knowing day time: my meals, the sun's movement on a cloudless day. It's hard not to know what time it is.

I would like to be bored here, to be tired of it, to want to go home. Each week we come, and before I've had enough of being here, it's time to go home.

One reason is that it's such a busy place; no not the household chores, simple amenities demand minimal work. Here, things special for me are nature's own, and she repairs and cleans and renews. A hole in the bedspread doesn't have to be repaired, it will grow only slowly, have other holes grow near it, until the demand is for a replacement—not a bright new one—but one that also feels used.

Nature always goes on. The sun casts shadows; the birds nest, raise young, come and go; the mouse visits; and the stream has its own seasons, its own ways.

The cabin here is part of the woods, and change is the rule here.

May 15, 1976

Rain is Coming

There's a promise of rain in the air, and a sense of expectation about its coming. The leaves are still; the stream has patterns reflecting an intermittent breeze.

Here, I shed a lot of ties with the outside world. The newspaper is unopened on the car seat. No radio. The binoculars show me the starlings caring for their screeching nestlings. Untouched are the brought books, letters to be answered. Links across time and space. I have barred the ordinary intrusions from my everyday world.

The birds are calling; the nasal humming of the nuthatches, the grackles, starling, crows are calling. The mallard pair are splashing in the backwater. The yellowed leaves of the holly fall; the redwing sings across the stream; the jenny wren tempts me to come and look for her nest.

The sky is greyer now. There's a rumbling of a spring rainstorm in the southwest.

May 15, 1976

Open Windows

The cabin was closed up when we arrived. The ordinary entrances and exits (doors and windows) were locked and shuttered. The openings used by mice, of course, remain year-round.

As I opened several windows, I unified the inside with the outside. Bird calls (an unfamiliar female oriole call or the usual chorus of crows, grackles, and redwings) are immediately inside. Breezes play on the leaves of the oaks and gums, and on the curtains.

The blue jay pair, silently sit on a cedar next to the hanging feeder. Their wings' beat telling me they're getting some snacks of grain. One jay jumps to a branch at the same height as the small hanging feeder, quickly poking the feeder to dislodge a few kernels, and jumps to the ground to eat. She doesn't try to eat a seed from the feeder, her target is the fallen seeds and she eats 3 or 4 quickly. Then she returns to the branch to jostle more seeds.

Here the border-line between "inside and outside" is fragile. Only three or four steps separate me from either door. The outside is inviting. I easily move in and out. As I sit here, the inside feels more like outside.

Throughout each day, the inside is not separate or self-sufficient. The toilet is out back, the wash water is out in the stream, the garbage pit is out in the woods, and we go to the woodshed for firewood.

The outside is central to our life here.

The cabin's outside is wood. Inside, the walls, ceilings, and floors are wood, the inside colors are brown. It's rooted in the woods.

May 16, 1987

Being Here

Sunday early afternoon. Though we are *here* in the fullest sense of the word, I know that in five or six hours we will leave to go "home." Each time I leave the cabin, I wish I were staying here.

I enjoy my life at home—my job, our friends, our garden, and the cultural resources so accessible there. Sid just told me that a fine ballet is in New York City, "a magical experience" the newspaper says. He thinks I'd like it, though he knows we are unlikely to see it.

Being here gives me time to think and write, and see the subtle seasonal changes in the woods and stream. I have often thought that I'd like to stay here until I'm bored. I'd like to stay until I'm fully "ready" to leave. I wonder: would I leave?

Surely I'd go back to see family and friends. There are celebrations of important human life events coming up next month: our son's college graduation, a family member's 60th birthday, friends' 40th anniversary, a young couple's wedding, as well as meetings of environmental and social justice organizations.

Yes, I'd go back to my home, go back to work in research and writing papers.

While I'm here, future plans are of little importance. Being here represents the *now.* Here, it is we who set the tempo of our days. We can get up early, dress, and then decide to go back to bed together. I can nap on the hammock.

We do keep a little list of garden chores for next week, or of things to bring down to the cabin when we return. Those lists, however, place an even stronger emphasis on the now. The future gets relegated to a scrap of paper.

May 16, 1987

The Clethra Is in Bloom

The white candle-like blooms of clethra are at their height this week. Near the entrance of the drive, the roadway is lined solidly with the shrubs, and in the shady understory the luminous flowers weave a loose white fabric over the cool green. The rich, sweet fragrance is heavy, kept in by the heavy roof of the 30 foot oaks and gum trees.

The stalks are crowds of half-inch wide five-petaled flowerets, often with oval white buds toward the tip. The fully open stalks are crawling with insects that resemble tiny lightning bugs each clinging to its own floweret for nectar. The dry brown stalk that will remain through winter into next spring begins to form toward the base where the faded flowerets drop off, leaving the swollen ovary and pistil to ripen in the coming weeks.

May 17, 1981

Plants and Me

I'm thinking of the trees, shrubs, plants around here. Now that it's spring, most of the leaves are coming out, though the sour gum has only tiny green buds and the sumac has no sign of green. I have a sense of comfort being amongst the plants. They have their cycles, their slow and sure ways. The spindly sweet gum sapling will sprout leaves, grow new branches, shed leaves, stand bare in the cold months. And it will do this with no input from me. Rather than my having to care for it, the sapling nourishes me. It doesn't move. Whenever I look there, it stands straight, motionless on a calm day. And with a bit of moving air, it sways ever so slightly, its leaves bobbing or quivering.

Last spring, I planted two Solomon's plumes from a distant trail, next to a post oak near the cabin. It's a member of the lily family, and I tried to get a root intact. Weekly this spring I've watched for it, and yet the plants where it had originally stood are now up over a foot. Maybe, it didn't survive the transplant, despite my frequent watering last summer. Yesterday, two tiny shoots of green appeared. I felt a sudden warm welcoming toward this new growth!

Down here, with acres of wild land, we still transplant weekly in the spring and fall. Sand myrtle now borders the outhouse trail, and dozens of plants are growing near us now, as a result of our digging and nurturing them over past seasons. Why? We like to see them, to watch them peek out of the ground, or note their tiny buds maturing into full leaf. The showy orchids are no more special than the climbing fern or willow oak.

Often a dead tree harbors some of its past strength and stands upright for years. The old pines on the burnt-over areas behind the vegetable garden are now leaden grey. A few are home to nesting birds, or offer a perch to a noisy brown thrasher. Each is a reminder of what has been, beyond the reach of my memory. Strange how a tree's life persists. Animals are fast to lose their flesh and decay. The cellulose in tree trunks is tightly packed, and perpetuates their viability. Even when a tree has fallen and is lichen-covered, the process of decay is slow.

There is a dynamism in plants. The terminal buds of the sour gum are pushing their green tips, leaves are there today where none were noted yesterday. I feel the subtle benign force in plants. The power in the living green plant is not found elsewhere.

Much of what we do here is being with plants—as they grow, leaf, and color and dry-up in the frosty autumn. Their constancy and stability provide quiet, enabling me to turn inward. The silence of plants pushes away the modern world.

Sand myrtle

May 18, 1996

After Hospital Intensive Care

Weeks ago, I had a raging, life-threatening pneumonia. During the nights of fit-full, sweaty, sleep—interrupted by nurses and respiratory therapists, as well as my careful maneuvering the tubes and wires. Sleep did not come as easily as it has most of my life.

Back then, I often thought of sitting in this chair, by the screened doors, overlooking the shimmering stream. This place is where so much joy and beauty have come to me, where I witness these pine barrens. It's so natural for me to be here.

Now, my breath comes easily; the laurel leaves shine in front of me; the sweet gum tree that we have trimmed yearly has seven clusters of not yet fully grown leaves. The ovenbird calls. The black and white warbler quietly whispers. The cardinal's loud call throbs. I'm watching the momentary fleeting of the yellow-throat pair through the underbrush below.

Could I have died, and never returned here to these familiar sights and sounds? If I had died these woods would not change. I am not a part of the woods. I only watch and listen. This place is eternal and I am ephemeral.

Although I have been away for 2 months, the cabin has stayed the same. The woods have changed with the spring weather, following the annual calendar.

My thoughts of the cabin from that hospital bed nurtured me along with the fluids going into my veins, and promised me a return to this chair, this calm sunny afternoon by the creek.

This place is a life force for me. I'm welcomed back. I'm at ease.

May 22, 1993

One Black Fly

As I came in the cabin door, a black fly clung to my shirt. That was over an hour ago. As I sat looking out the window—through the gum trees and the newly leafing laurel, past the birdfeeder with an occasional titmouse or chickadee, I saw the sky-blue stream shimmering in the afternoon light. Then I looked out at the old post oak, past the nest box with cotton stuffing most of the opening. I realized that no wren has chosen to nest there this spring.

When I looked back toward the stream my eye caught the movement of a tiny black speck, flying and walking on the window glass as if it were trying to get outside: the black fly. In the past, I've seen black flies crawling up the inside of the door screen, and I've squashed the insect with my finger. There are hordes of these tiny flies outside now. They bite once in a while. At first, I can't even feel a bite, but soon a drop of blood may appear, and for the next seven days (until I return to the cabin to get another few bites) there is a red itch, a nagging scab that once rubbed bleeds again, scabs again, itches again and the seven-day cycle continues.

This black fly was different—I had lazily brought her inside. I should have brushed her off my sleeve. So, I went for the plastic cup and the thin 3 inch metal square that stay on the step to the attic. They are used to capture unwelcome insects and return them to the outside. Usually, these are white-faced hornets that insist on living here with us. They are generally docile, but they are moody and we have been stung several times.

I waited for the tiny fly to move to the center of the glass pane to capture it. When I released it outside, it barely moved. Maybe, it had been crushed by the cup closing down on the metal. I doubted that it could fly again.

The little creature was maimed or killed, and clumsily I did it. Regardless of my good intentions, the world goes on. The great crested flycatcher is calling, but he won't miss that tiny morsel. The chickadee is taking still another sunflower seed from the feeder. My dinner is on the stove. Yet, the world has one less black fly.

When each of us live and die the world changes. Other creatures continue to eat and to live.

May 22, 1993

Spring Energy

Spring is full of energy. Small tan moths symbolize spring's fullness of life, its amazing urge toward growth. Almost with abandon, leaves grow quickly, pollen spreads widely, larvae morph into small flying angels. They hold onto life for their allotted time. Each has a promise of regeneration in next year's spring, but none survive to see their progeny. Although green pine needles survive our cold winters, they, too, drop off in coming seasons as new needles replace them.

May 22, 1993

Red Squirrel

A red squirrel has built a nest of grasses, paper, cotton threads and fringe from our pillows and coverlets. It's nested right outside our bedroom window, next to the closed old wooden shutter. Roughly the nest measures over a foot long and five to six inches high, about enough to fill a large shoe box. Watching this fluffy pile has occupied us for several hours. We had been hoping that the secretive animal might be a flying squirrel which is nocturnal. So last night at dusk for almost an hour, we watched as there was sporadic movement toward one end. As our room became quite dark, I thought (imagined) I saw a tan head, but the animal kept hidden. We hoped it would scurry to the top of the shutter and skim off into the night. Rather it quieted down and probably slept when we did. We heard nothing during the night, but at 6:45 this morning a red squirrel stretched full length along the window jam and ran up the shutter and left. But the fluff continued to move after the animal left—*a family!*

Our books on wildlife tell little about squirrel family behavior, except that this species lives mostly in evergreen woods (our pitch pine suits them), eats cones and leaves the cores, nests twice a year, has one to seven young, gestation 40–45 days.

The squirrels' behavior is a mystery to us. What's in the nest? Is the female staying here while the male forages? How many young are there? We are permitted to have half a look. But we can't see into the nest. We periodically peek and wonder.

The whole of our woods is like this red squirrel's nest. We are close, we can see mysterious things.

There are now scores of small, tan moths that flit from leaves after they land a few seconds. We don't know anything about their larvae: what they eat, yet they reappear this time every spring. And the male yellow throat that has been around our dooryard, does it have a nest nearby on the ground? And the phoebe who built half of a nest on our porch that a wind or an animal pushed off its shelf, is now back again, has the phoebe returned to rebuild?

We only get half a look at our world in these woods. The mystery of the squirrel's nest is the mystery of the woods. I'm glad we can see part of it. Each new glimpse is a surprise, and an invitation to watch ever more carefully.

May 23, 1987

Strangers

Rarely, less than once a year, a stranger drives in. It's a shock to see an unknown car in our clearing. Most of the time it's a visitor to a nearby cabin, "lost." Our sand lane just runs a few hundred yards from the paved road, and then stops at our cabin. It's not a through lane to anywhere. The only way out is back the way you came in.

Once a young couple appeared, probably looking for a private spot. Another couple zoomed in on a motorcycle, "Looking for the main road," they said. We hope they're not vandals or thieves. We don't look with pleasure on strangers—we see this as *our* place.

Once a middle-aged couple drove in. His family had owned the place before we bought it, and he remembered many happy times here, and wanted to show his friend. We enjoyed their visit, his reminiscing, and pointing out special things around the cabin.

Several times we've arrived at the cabin, and noted tire tracks or other signs that strangers had been here while we were away. As we round the last bend in the lane, I often hope we'll find things just as we left them—at least free from human interference.

We've had two break-ins and robberies—canoes, kerosene heater, tools, sleeping bags taken. Police think that things were sold at nearby flea markets. They're certainly lost to us.

Shortly before our last robbery, as our full-time neighbor was driving into the lane, she saw a pickup truck with a canoe on its way out. The driver explained that his son had left his canoe along the stream and he had just picked it up. When she got home she discovered that he had stolen her canoe.

The things in our cabin, though they're functional, attractive and we're used to them, are not especially important to me. They don't represent family keepsakes, childhood memories. They are not irreplaceable. What is important is the cabin itself: we have spent many days here—we know the woods, the plants, the stream, the backwater, the trails.

It's a special place, not one that abides strangers.

May 23, 1987

Both Hands

If it weren't for Lou and Eileen Hand, we may never have come to spend our time in these Pine Barrens. About 15 years ago, we had certainly heard of the area, and on an outing to a nature center in Batsto, miles from here, we saw a small sign about a botany trip on the Wading River. We signed up for the day trip.

The Hands were the leaders. Eileen is a natural teller of tales, her Irish accent and quick wit made it fun to listen. She told of their stream, neighbors who had rented to a minister who spent much of the time with youngsters—in the nude. The tale went on—neighbors objecting to the goings on in that cabin, and eventually the minister had to vacate.

I was most interested in the word "rented." I asked for the name of the owner of their nearby cabin, and though I was warned that the minister episode might deter any further rentals, we phoned the Paulmiers. Yes, they would consider renting their cabin for the summer. They liked the idea that we'd use the place most every weekend, to deter vandals. We paid a few hundred dollars, and shortly found ourselves neighbors upstream from the Hands.

Lou and Eileen were retired. He had worked, and they had lived most of their married life, in northeast Philadelphia. Both are naturalists—Lou the preeminent botanist in the pine barrens. He knew each plant, its habitat, its special characteristics—and he enjoyed talking about plants, at length. We liked to listen. We were full of questions and enthusiastically looked forward to each encounter with Lou and Eileen. Over the years, we'd visit back and forth, share meals, and take walks together.

Once when they came to the cabin for dinner and a walk, Lou had told us the name of a solidago (goldenrod). The next day he thought better of it and sent us a note correcting the identification. I used to keep specimens of unknown flora pressed,

54

awaiting our next meeting. I was so pleased to learn the name of a new flower or shrub, or to find that my "new" plant was a specimen of something quite familiar.

On one of our last visits to them in their house down our stream, they gave us a 1910 botany of the Pine Barrens. In Lou's clear, neat hand, the inscription read: "Best wishes to Sid & Miriam Moss for many happy years in the field for enjoying the interest & beauty of our Pine Barren plants. Both Hands, Eileen & Louis July 2, 1983."

Over the years, we were sad to see Lou's vitality ebb, 'til he could no longer tramp the woods. Eileen nursed and cared for him until she went beyond her endurance, and now Lou lives in a nursing home.

Last time we visited him (two years ago) we took a vase of wildflowers which he seemed to enjoy and recognize. Without Eileen's encouragement we haven't returned. Eileen will be 79 on Monday—she is active, now she lives alone in a ranch house in a retirement community.

We've gone on pine barrens field trips with several people, and enjoyed each, but going even a few steps with Both Hands was the greatest pleasure. He enjoyed sharing, was patient, seemed to tell as much as you wanted to know.

How I'd like to walk in these woods again with Lou and Eileen Hand.

May 26, 1985

Backwater Welcome

As we walked the loop trail to the Evans (trimming the oaks, clethra, smilax), I saw subtle shifts in new growth since last fall.

Now, we return to our backwater. Here the water cools my feet, and the bright green narrow leaves of iris welcome me. One blue iris is in full bloom, the first I've seen this May. Its veined patterns are delicate and fragile. I know that next week the nearby buds will open. These earliest blossoms are especially welcome. They fulfill the promise of spring.

May 28, 1987

We Don't Live Here Alone

Again a field mouse has been living here—probably coming in through the normal route under the refrigerator. When we arrived yesterday there were a half dozen ¼″ black droppings on the kitchen countertop, and soap shavings in the ceramic soap dish.

Earlier this year I had put my hand right into a marvelous ball of fluff, in the pot-holder basket on top of the refrigerator. It was surely a mouse nest made of strands of potholder stuffing, with an inch-wide cavity lined with fine grey mouse hairs. We have a havahart trap. We can put some peanut butter or cheese on a lever, which when touched by the mouse closes the escape door at each end. Mice must be nocturnal, because we've set traps during the day (even when we've been out for quite a while) but only at night do mice get caught.

At 4 or 5 a.m., a small rattley noise awakened me. I turned to Sid and said, "a mouse is in the trap." "It's been there a half-hour," he replied. On and off during my sleep, I could hear that tinkling rattle. The mouse moving around the trap, crouching back under the slanting metal doors.

Now the tiny critter is shivering in fear. Trap is sitting on newspaper (scared mice urinate and defecate a lot). There are 86 turds on the newspaper and a dozen more in the trap. We'll put it near the table while we eat breakfast. After a while, Sid will take the trap down the road a mile or so, and release the mouse.

Looking at the tiny mouse, I feel remote and powerful. Remote in the sense that although my eyes are only a few inches from hers, I know nothing about her life, the rhythm of her day—whether she has nestlings or young somewhere awaiting her—or if she is a "he."

I do feel that mouse has little control over her whereabouts right now. She's in a pretty secure trap, with no way of chewing out, no holes in the wire large enough for more than her foot. I'm a jailer. I set the trap. I have the mouse in it. I can try to feel benign about my plan to remove mouse from this cabin, but she may have a family (or may be a newly grown young one herself). I've become a predator, as if I'm a large bird, sweeping down. Will she continue to live "normally," after being taken a mile down the road?

I catch and move mouse at my convenience with little thought for mouse.

I'm trying to think of a human analogy to this situation. Nazis and the holocaust? Hungry Africans living in relocation camps? Japanese Americans during WWII? In each situation the caged victims had little or no choice, and once caught in the system, the holes in the wire were too small for escape. The captors had all the power over life or death. Yet my personal daily life goes on as usual.

Now, Sid and I have examined each other for ticks. He is watering the garden. I glance up at the wren's insistent call to see if he has finally enticed a female to settle into a nest. The tea kettle boils.

Meanwhile, the mouse crouches in the trap.

May 28, 1978

Listening

Listening now, I heard the pencil rub its lead into the words on this page; the brush of denim against denim as I cross and re-cross my legs. My hand sliding across the paper. And now I hear my own breath—the rhythmic inhale and exhale.

I listen now to the blue jays' cry, the flickers' bleat, the red wings' chortle, the pewees' whine. These are easy to hear.

When I concentrate on the birds' calls, awareness of my breath is gone. As I focus on the sound of the pattern of my breathing, the outer world recedes.

I want to see the bird on wing and not ignore the fly on my hand. I want to know the sound of my own feet along the path. Each part of my world here has an important song.

Swamp Azalea

May 29, 1994

Transplanting Blue-Eyed Grass

We drove to nearby Whitesbog today. The azaleas were coming into bloom, their fragrance was heavy and sweet. Although the edges of the sand lanes are cut back, the azaleas thrive. A small one brushed my leg as I walked along. Sid tried to dig it up so we could transplant it near the cabin, but the root was large and went deep. We left it in its place.

We did dig up a clump of blue-eyed grass that we hope will thrive in our door yard.

Finally, we saw a lone plant of golden club. It seemed in the midst of a place where small row boats and canoes are launched. Barefooted Sid, again, found the roots went deep, and the plant remains there.

Over the years we have brought local plants to our place—few have thrived. Bearberry, gerardia, pine barrens sand wort, orange milk wort, orchis. We carefully put each plant in a place that we judged would be similar to where we found it. None of these flourished. There were other failures: cardinal flower, shortia . . .

But then there were our successes: wild lily of the valley, birds foot violets, butterfly bush, Saint Andrews cross—and arbutus. Each has taken hold. Year after year they thrive and we enjoy them.

We try to dig up and take plants that are plentiful where we find them, and only plants that are in habitats like ours. If the blue-eyed grass fails, we'll not try it again.

We'd not try to move an animal, bird or insect or mammal here. Why with relative abandon do we transplant flora? Again, I think we have less basic regard for plants. It is as if plants were not as important as animals . . . as if their survival hardly matters.

May 29, 1988

We Rearrange Our World . . .

The woods around the cabin include mostly pines, sweet gum, sour gum, and sassafras. Down in the wetter areas near streamside are cedar—Sid's favorite.

Over the years we've transplanted cedar seedlings to be near the cabin. Nine years ago, we placed one on either side of the propane tanks. Now, one is less than 3 feet tall; its main stem snapped off years ago, and it never resumed its growth. The other is tall, way up twelve to fourteen feet.

For four to five years, three cedar seedlings have been struggling to survive up near the outhouse. Each season an inch or two of new cedar growth is added, but none are a foot tall yet. A five foot cedar stands straight, between the screen porch and a big pine. It stands just a few feet from another cedar which has barely reached eight inches.

Our efforts to plant cedar are like our efforts to arrange our social world. Some of our seedlings take hold—even more than we had wished; others don't flourish at all. Perhaps the soil does not provide the nourishment they need.

New friends or acquaintances over a lifetime may resist taking root alongside us. Some reach out to us warmly, sometimes more eagerly than we had anticipated. For many friends there is an easy give and take, each being in tune with the wishes and expectations of the other. There are also disappointments, of new ties cut short, perhaps what I saw as mutuality was simply not there. Most painful are the old ties that shrivel; one world has clearly become two separate spheres. Only the past offers the glue; the future holds little promise.

We can plan, and rearrange—but friendships and plants grow as they will.

View across stream

May 30, 1977

Being in This Place

The orchard oriole built a nest over the dock last year, and raised a brood and left. And yesterday, as I looked at the ball of grasses hanging from the pine tree it seemed as if it was refurbished.

Now as I sit here, I have seen the male, and then the female. They are back to use their nest again. My eyes have filled with tears. The tug of home, of the familiar, is strong for the oriole . . . and for me.

Our old friend has often said that he can't long stay away from his "area" in Maine. When he first said it, I thought it was a nice idea. I had thought of my suburban community, and wondered if the social ties that I have there are analogous to what he meant.

Then we began to come down to the pine barrens. Now, for five years, most every week all year round we're here. I have a strong tie with this place. It's quiet and open, it's fresh and alive here. It's always the same, and it's always new: There is always a new flower, a colony of beaver, a chipmunk family, a summer nest of mice in a lime sack next to the canoe.

I have come to know this place gradually. Each visit lets me see more . . . and more of myself, too.

A place must be savored, a place must be revisited. One must have time to be in a place, to wander, to look, to feel. It takes a long time to know a place.

May 30, 1977

Ripples

The breeze brings ripples to skim the top of the stream. And then the ripples die down for a quiet spell.

This breeze is part of the cosmos. Man can predict only grossly how and when it will blow. We cannot guess whether the upstream gust will shift at any moment. The petals and the dry leaves from last fall float along, their ultimate path is downstream, but the breeze may push them to the side or delay their drift.

The water bugs are undeterred. They dart along the stream margin, making a pattern in their wake. A fish comes up to get a snack, and now an ever-widening set of circles spreads, until a moment later it's all calm. Again a water bug darts across, leaving a wedge of ripples, soon to disappear.

The stream flows on. Its surface is all we see. The brown water clothes the naked swimmer and hides the sandy bottom. The ripples and the patterns are fleeting, though their pattern is clear and definite now, in an eye's blink they disappear— smoothed over.

Is the stream of life ever changed by ephemeral ripples?

May 30, 1977

Joy in Doing

Is there an innate quality we have to "show and tell"? The female redwing blackbird began to make her nest in a clethra bush across the stream yesterday. And now, every few minutes she returns with a beak full of grasses and twigs. She weaves them in, shapes the nest and then flies off low over the stream with a loud, reverberating cry that seems to affirm what she's just done: another layer, another step to nest completion.

Perhaps other birds do slip quietly off the nest as they build it, but this redwing certainly doesn't. She's made four noisy flights out since I began to write. Such energy! She's working hard, and she repeatedly proclaims "Another layer of nest!" to the world.

Are humans so different? As we work or study, or do our daily tasks, we do get a joy in declaring our achievements. Not to get ascendancy over someone else, not to call attention to our power and might, but to cry out the simple satisfaction in our work.

There are few among us who create a work of art for ourselves alone. Like the redwing, we do affirm our work, as it is in progress or when it is complete, proclaiming its existence and announcing our creativity.

Are we too achievement-oriented? I think that is the human condition. Not that I must create what is dictated by others; not that I must create a "thing" but that I must work and use myself through time to some purpose. And further, as the redwing, that I proclaim what I am doing.

Is this what the bird and I call affirming ourselves?

June 1, 1984

Raining

Several times today the sky darkened and it was raining. Then the drops came down the chimney, but not enough to put out the paper trash fire. Otherwise the rain is outside—and even with the big screen doors open facing the stream, the rain has not splashed in.

Bird songs stop during the showers, or are the songs drowned out by the raindrops? The thin green-black damselfly continues its flights, from the sweet gum to the laurel.

The stream is dark grey-brown, edged with small blueberry leaves.

As the shower thins out, the wren begins his bubbly song. He's enticing the female to nest again, but this time they may move from the nest box on the post oak outside our window, to another spot nearby.

Now the rain has stopped, but the drops roll off the leaves, off the branches, onto other leaves, and to the under story of bushes with their dusty blue fruit.

It's raining again. I watch a rosette of sour gum leaves on an outstretched branch. It stands quite immobile, until one or another of its leaves is touched by a raindrop and it quivers downward, then returns to its former position. With harder sheets of rain, the rosette still maintains its upright stance, though the six individual leaves jerk down and back up in their own rhythm.

Dozing off . . . . .

June 5, 1987

Cutting Trails with Esther

We usually cut our trails in early spring or late fall, when the branches have no leaves. Then we can snip off the twigs, toss them a few yards off the trail, and leave little trace of our work. But somehow this time of late spring forces us to cut once again. New growth surges over two week's time, and even our most used paths to outhouse and garbage pit become partially obscured. If we fail to trim, we get soaked when we walk after rains or heavy dew. Also, we attract more ticks as we brush by the blueberry and laurel leaves.

Some of the paths had been here when we first came. A few were clear. Others we followed only by picking our way from one old strip of rag to another. Esther, our neighbor down the lane, came by. Now, past her mid-eighties, she's lived alone in her cabin for several decades. Esther is our closest companion in the Pine Barrens. She introduced us to the rhythm of daily living in the natural world here. Her feet somehow followed along old paths. Her eyes were more attuned to tell-tale cuts. She marked the trails with new strips of rag.

In some ways paths are reassuring. They invite us to stroll along, and make us feel that we belong in this wild place. We tread and re-tread the trails—sometimes venturing a few yards off to explore, but mostly carefully noting the familiar trees, shrubs, logs along the way.

In other ways, I feel that cutting a path is a sacrilege. The woods belong to stay as they are, and I should intrude as little as possible. We have some "rules" about trimming: we try not to cut pines, laurels—and yet clip oaks and blueberries with little concern. It's as if there are more and less worthy shrubs, and our calculus values evergreens more than the fast-growing deciduous oaks and blueberries.

June 8, 1991

Bird Mothers & Their Young

Most all of the birds we're seeing around the cabin now are probably nesting—raising their young. We've put up a small platform on the side of the screened porch for the phoebe—and this is the first year we've been around to see five tiny hatchlings. Mother bird often sits on her nest as we carefully go back and forth, coming within arm's length of her.

The wren family is further along. Last week they may have hatched, and now they squeak and chirp as mother bird goes into the nest box, and they quiet down after she flies out with the fecal sack.

Bird-rearing seems so simple from where I sit. There are no books, classes, or observations of role models. It comes quite naturally to parent and offspring. Nestlings stay in their nest and are regularly fed until they can fly off. The nest must get more crowded as the new born changes from the size of a small cherry to a pretty full-grown bird. Parents continue to feed for a time after the young take wing. Much seems to be instinctual for both generations. I wonder how many of the young survive until the next spring nesting time.

How different from the human species, where even the birthing process is a social experience. After nine months, there are human helpers around. And then there is a long period of dependence. Human infants can't be left in a nest 'til they fledge, they must be tended night and day. Once they're off to school, they return home for protection and nurturance for many years.

Is there any comparison between bird mothers/fathers and human parents. We seem to think that children retain a strong tie to parents over the life cycle, even into the child's old age when the parent has died. For a bird, how does it work? With little or nothing of what we call "culture" perhaps the young bird becomes independent in a matter of weeks, and no longer is tied to its parents. Do parents lead young birds in migration, or do each go independently to more hospitable climes?

If a young bird, several weeks out of the nest, is hurt, would the parent bird note it any more than the parent would note any other hurt young bird? The human parent is always concerned about the wellbeing of their human child, even to planning for inheritance and other support after the parent dies.

The other day, I read that perhaps there is an animal model of bereavement: initial sadness and missing the other, and then getting on with life. Is that a preferable response to long persistent sadness and feelings of loss experienced by humans. What is the bird's pattern?

Lady Slippers

June 10, 1979

Lady Slipper

The lady slipper orchid is a beautiful spring flower. It's a treasure found along the trailside and in the woods here. I had hoped to find a lady slipper on the grounds near the cabin. What a joy when the pair of leaves of one appeared next to our parked car. No bud or flower came forth, but I treasure it and I will keep it clear and well marked so that it may grow for future years.

Each time we've walked along our trails, or cut or trimmed trails, I looked about, and lo, along the road into camp, I discovered three or four of the orchids, either too small to bloom, or already past this year's bloom. The closest was near the cabin, a few feet off the path.

Today, I found a large pair of leaves a few yards past the woodshed, only a matter of inches from the trail we walk weekly. How could my eyes have missed it before? And then off the path to the outhouse, only a few yards from our front door, tucked under some brush, standing full and tall, a bloom stalk withered from last month's flower, the largest, most robust plant of all.

Nearer to home the more beauty I find. Looking for beauty in far places, or even remote trails, yields less than searching just beyond arm's reach.

Tsu Hause ist Beste

June 14, 1986

"Finding" the Shadbush

It was the week of the shadbush bloom and Sid and I had transplanted a few cedar seedlings from off the garden trail to up near the cabin. A while later that day—I walked back to the brush pile and "found" a very large shadbush. I'd never known it was there, but soon realized that it was easily viewed from the outhouse seat.

One must look for things "in their time." When a shadbush is not in bloom it is not notable—it stands alone masked among the scrub oak and maples. But in bloom it makes me catch my breath. It's here, it's part of our place, and I never knew.

Now, into early summer, that section of the woods is so different from the way it was in past Junes. Now I know that the shadbush is there. I can say, "It's up by the big shadbush." I can expect, next spring, to see it full of white blooms again.

There are so many hidden parts of ourselves and our dear ones—but they too are hidden, and if I'm not open to seeing them at unexpected times and contexts, I'll miss finding them. I won't know about them at all.

Sid inside cabin

SUMMER

Cabin in Summer

June 16, 1985

Sitting and Listening

It's quiet. I'm just sitting and listening. Last night's rain left crystal balls on every leaf, and at the tip of each pine needle. The sounds of water dripping mix with droppings of gypsy moths. Their fat, slow-moving larvae cling to the underside of many leaves, as they munch their way to their chrysalis stage.

The cuckoo and the great crested flycatcher intermittently intrude their calls on the silence. The wren parent bubbles in song from dawn to dusk on its repeated flights to feed the newly hatched birdlets. A large awkward young grackle flutters noisily on a dead branch over the stream to get an extra feeding from its parent. A raucous jay is calling out every second or two from the top of a nearby pine; the catbird is close with its mewing. Intermittent single notes from the towhee come from just below the screen door that overlooks the stream. The crow, cawing as it flies over the bend in the stream, continues to call as it goes downstream.

A lot that's happening is going on in silence. The nestlings in the wren box are quiet; the eastern painted turtle crawled under leaves and is mute; the Fowler's toad is nowhere to be seen.

What do all these sounds and silences have to do with me? In a way they bound my world. The living things in the woods are my nest. They are the structures on which I lay my thoughts, or no, they become entwined in my thoughts. Whether I'm here or not, the wren family will nest. I am the voyeur, the outsider, watching, listening. What I observe, draws me in, and tells me about my world in these woods. The lives of these birds are comforting, reassuring. The simple rhythm of nesting takes me away from schedules and obligations, into the core my own life. Perhaps it lets me peel off everyday expectations—and just sit here.

June 18, 1993

First Dip of the Summer

First dip of the summer was late this afternoon. Before that we took the rag rug upstairs, along with the guard we keep on the floor in front of the wood stove, and we carried down the straw rug we brought from our Dominica trip. Also, Sid climbed onto the porch roof, and cut back pine branches too close to the cabin.

The stream has changed our dock area. There's a new sand bar around our entry into the stream. The water level is low. Sid tossed away a number of twigs and branches that now stick out of the sand in the shoulder-deep water.

I left my clothes in the house and walked in where the current pulls the cooling water around the curve. Then I swam upstream a few yards to the shallow sandy area where I could float while my hands held onto the sandy bottom. With gentle kicking I could stay in one place, wetting my face, blowing some bubbles in the tea-colored stream.

Everything is green, with only subtle color differences between the leaves of blueberries, gum trees, clethra, and grasses. I pay little attention to the distinct hue of each plant because I look for leaf shape and the configuration of the bushes to distinguish between them. Without my glasses the world becomes flattened—dark stems, trunks, and branches intertwined within the mottled green.

I feel the cool stream against my bare body. It's a familiar welcome feeling so different from being in the ocean, when I wear a bathing suit, and the tender touch of water is lost.

June 25, 1993

Dead Trees across the Stream

Year after year, dead trees form familiar landmarks. Some have fallen to link the two banks, and they rise and fall from view as the water level changes. This morning the big pine upstream is so far above the water that we can barely touch it with a reaching arm. Previous times, we've crouched low in the canoe to be sure we clear it.

Most days the trunk of another tree is enough underwater to permit us to glide over, hardly noticing it. Today we easily pass under its arched end.

The sour gums' delicate branches, just beyond the huge tilting willow oak, form a jeweled green canopy.

Occasionally a new tree falls, and someone eventually comes by to saw a passageway. Large cut trunks often lie submerged. As the water level shifts, our canoe can get caught up on a log.

On our left, in deep water as the stream turns right, is a slow-growing cedar/lichen garden. The seedlings are only a few inches high, amid red tipped pale cladonia. I guess there is just the barest amount of organic material to sustain these plants. Maybe the wood from the long dead tree is releasing some of its energy.

It's reassuring to see the dead trees, the logs, and to canoe over or past them. They mark the way, providing boundaries of our path upstream and downstream. They represent the past in the present. They are solid reality, not vague or ephemeral. I see them directly, not through a veil of memory.

This morning, as we canoed downstream from Greenwood bridge, we let the current carry us along, only paddling to avoid a log or maneuver a curve, or to remove a couple discarded cans or bottles lodged along the side.

The dead trees in the stream are like people in my past. Always there, solid, providing some boundaries to our path as we go on the stream of life. They have in small ways transformed my world as I enjoy the beauty of the underwater cedar/lichen garden.

I feel stronger as I manage my way through these old dead trees. Someday I will be one of them. Others will pass by.

Sand lane in fog

July 2, 1993

Constancy and Change

Each summer week, when I first go down the trails next to the cabin, I walk through cobwebs—thin, hardly felt except against my bare skin. Over the days since our last visit each animal has continued its daily life, and inevitably a few spiders have crossed the trail with their gossamer nets. Thin cobwebs across my trail symbolize complex tales of change.

It's a reminder to me that this place has a life of its own, and in between our visits the insects, spiders, birds, small furry mammals are active. As I go crashing through the thin strands built up over days or weeks, I fail to see and feel the world as it has become, and I think this place has stayed just as it was in my last visit.

Of course, I am sensitive to the newly blooming seasonal flowers. I see the hummingbird feeder is empty, a fern has unfolded at full height on the trail, or a deer has left a hoof print and dug a small hole. But overall, I see this place as a constant, as the way it has been over time.

I don't see the infinite small changes: a lichen-crusted twig broken, a few ends of pine branches chewed off, remnants of pine cones after the red squirrel carefully ate each seed, a new insect in a spider's large flat web.

These constancy themes recur when I see a family member, a neighbor or friend after a lapse of days or months. I look for constancy. I want to be with the same person whom I have known in past. If I notice changes, I have to decide whether this is a temporary, a transitory characteristic, or whether I will have to integrate these changes into my view of the real person. I can classify some as temporary: minor illness, lapse of memory, hair tightly curled after a permanent, an unexpected response. The person is unchanged. Oft repeated instances of these events may lead to a question of continuity and I may allow for some change, some difference.

Whether I am interacting with the environment here at the cabin or with another person, I hold onto the constancy. Perhaps, I learn to develop a range of events and behaviors that I consider ordinary, and reflective of basic stability. When things occur that are out of that range, they are a threat to my view of a person or the world, and I shift to consider a new perspective.

Pine branch

July 2, 1988

Returning to the Cabin

As we drove to the cabin, I was unsure how comfortable I would feel back here. I wanted to be here, but I'm not sure. That "but" was never a word that would follow my wish to be at the cabin on a beautiful summer weekend.

The last week or so had been different. It had been enough to make a change in my expectations of life here. I had "flu-like" symptoms of what may be nothing, or what may be Lyme disease. Three weeks after having two tick bites, I had fever and fatigue that kept me in bed all of last weekend. These past days have been spent with much emphasis on ticks, tick bites, and Lyme disease. I made trips to the doctor, phone calls to Yale University Hospital to inquire about diagnosis and treatment.

We were concerned. Could we enjoy our cabin as we always have or would a deep new fear take hold of us? After all, these tiny, ubiquitous ticks are a threat to our health.

In order to find ticks on our clothing, we habitually wear long white pants (tucked into white socks), long sleeved shirts, repellent—when we go out to walk the trails, cut brush, or when we go to the garden, the garbage pit, the outhouse. We continue to take precautions. Can we relax today and do as we wish?

Somehow, I sense that little has changed. The canoe trip upstream was, as always, different from any before. The stream has a way of changing its face with the weather and season. The water level is very low, yet there were no obstructing logs on the stream bottom, and no trees had fallen across the snaking ribbon of brown to block our way.

The ripening wild blueberries stood in the sun along the stream—and offered us our first taste of sweet summer. A few heavily fragrant azaleas remained in bloom—

most of the world was green-leaved shrubs. The clethra (sweet pepper bush) has green spires which will bloom white in a few weeks.

Now, in the afternoon, as I look through the layers of branches, I see that the sweet gum stems are brushed yellow green, the laurel ovals are blue green, the sour gum petals are pale, the post oak leaves are dark, and the maples across the stream have a purple tinge. Subtle differences of shade and value, yet the overall view is green—marked throughout by deep brown twigs and branches holding up the hues of green.

The cabin is the same—my anxiety seems to have been smoothed over by the comfort of this beautiful place. Almost to reassure us, this first full day has ended with our having found only one large dog tick, and no disease-carrying tiny deer ticks.

The pink clouds reflect the sunset's glow, against the blue sky. The breezes of earlier today have moved away. The fragile leaves are held motionless in the cool evening air.

I'm comfortable and I belong here.

July 4, 1977

So Much Life Around

This is what I observe when I am sitting next to the stream in the morning.

Across in the backwater is a black backed turtle, about 6″ in diameter.

Four or five yards across the stream, three feet up in the blueberry bush is a chipmunk, munching the first ripe berries.

Crouched on a branch of a clethra bush, swaying in the mid-day breeze, is a young but not very small redwing blackbird. Shielded from the sun by the overhanging leaves, clutching the small branch as it stretches its wings (one at a time), it awaits the sleek father's trip with an insect.

Criss-crossing the stream, in patterns which seem random to me, are water bugs, leaving parallel ripples in the V-shaped wakes.

Under my right thigh is a tick, drawn to the warmth of my body. I flick him off.

Earlier the catbird pair landed side by side on a branch a yard from me, looked at me for an instant, and flew off together. Now I hear a rustling in the underbrush, and see a catbird emerge—a nest?

The slim blue and green brilliant damselflies dart, then rest. The large white-bodied/black-winged dragonfly returns nearby throughout the morning. Is this his hunting ground?

The frog, twangs twice to its mate, a few yards downstream.

A kingbird perches on a broken lower branch of a dying sweet gum tree. Beaver work of two summers past is seen all along this stream. The kingbird launches off after a bug, returns to the perch to watch and wait again.

Two damselflies, in tandem, briefly land on Sid's book, and fly off together.

A pair of large black dragonflies perch a foot apart, then fly off in a wild chase of each other.

The Carolina wren is singing loudly. She nervously approaches and flies onto the old swamp maple. A few low squeaks and she flies off. She returns again, a fat insect in her beak. Now I hear the quiet "twerp." The nest is hardly five feet from where I sit. When she flies away, she starts to sing—and sing! Intermingled with her song is the red wing's and flicker's, and the frog's twang.

Grasses in stream

July 8, 1988

Our Screens

Our window screens stand between us and the outside—they sharply reduce the insects in the cabin. The gypsy moths, mosquitoes, deer flies, and ticks, as well as birds, mice and lizards are generally kept out.

Otherwise, the sun, the breezes, the air circulate into and through the cabin. Through the screens we can see out to the sky, the trees, the stream. I know that I am sitting *inside* (on an upholstered chair, my feet on the rag rug), yet the real *outside* is here.

There is no TV or computer screen as a proxy for the outside. The woods are here, framed by the tall cedars along the stream. When the breeze flutters, it jostles the sweet gum leaves, I feel the brush of air.

Today on public radio, a commentator was bemoaning the way that screens are removing us from the physical and inter-personal reality of our worlds. It is the TV and the computer screen she was talking about.

To me, the reality of a screen erases the reality of the objective world. We see a government official or TV news analyst talking directly and spontaneously to us (and forget that he or she is dressed, lighted, practiced to appear talking directly to us). Yet s/he's never *seen* us, *heard* us, nor does s/he expect to have a one-to-one interaction with us. The screen on which the person appears has detached the person from our real world.

Earlier this week a US ship captain shot down an Iranian commercial passenger plane, killing almost 300 people. He had not been able to distinguish on his computer screen between the huge airbus and a small fighter plane of the military.

This spring, Dad wrote a letter to a presidential candidate—his illness was made so real by the TV that Dad wrote a real letter wishing him a speedy recovery. Was he writing a letter to the screen?

Even when we travel to a distant place there are screens—of language, of unknown local ways, of so many unfamiliar people, buildings, roads, flora and fauna. What can we see? Are there any ways other than repeated experiences in a place that will help to pierce the screen?

Sweetgum leaf

July 9, 1989

Inside and Outside

In warm weather, we eat at a round table on our screened porch. We have a wooden floor under our feet, and a shingled roof over our head. In the morning we have the early sun, backlighting the goldenrods, wild indigo, pines, and oaks. In mid-day, it's all shade here—and toward day's end, the sun comes in on the stream side. Are we "inside" or "outside"? In my dogged way, I insist that we are *both*.

What is it about our way of thinking—whether it be common parlance or social science theory—that insists on a series of binary themes and concepts? Why can't I be inside *and* outside? Why does the world tug on me to choose: inside *or* outside?

Why can't I be patient and impatient? Our most impatient friend, Bob, is mightily patient in his careful teaching and, his meticulous surgery. I see him as a patient and impatient man.

As I sit here in the porch, I really am outside. I'm only an arms-length away from laurel and sweet fern and from the blueberry bushes. The breeze out here is cooling. The window into the kitchen lets me reach in and put dishes in the sink to be washed, or to refill a glass of ice tea. I am inside.

My life is full of what some would say are contradictions, and what I perceive to be many perspectives. Some dimensions may have tension with others. I know I am now inside *and* outside the cabin.

I accept the duality.

July 16, 1989

Focus on the Small

Since Esther died, Nan, a young woman in her early twenties, has been renting Esther's house down the lane. Last night Nan walked over—barefoot with her dog Cedar—pushing an old wheelbarrow full of her sensitive, more-than-life-size art. She hopes one day to put her paintings together for a book. She says she paints on a large scale because she has so much to say about small things. For her senior art project in college, one of her pieces, about her family's farm, was a goat's udder.

I feel she's a kindred soul. My best photographs of nature have always looked closely at the small. I've often focused to see a special pattern or image. I find that looking at one leaf at a time helps me to feel close to the woods.

July 20, 1996

We're Here Alone

My time at the cabin is not a social time. We rarely have guests here, less than once a year. Neighbors rarely stop by. Since Esther died, Jim, from next cottage, is our most frequent visitor.

There's little time spent in talking with others. We might see an occasional canoe on the stream. Today, a couple went by. I had never seen them before, perhaps they were visiting someone nearby. The man said, "Is your power on?" As they passed by I said, "We never had any power, so it's not going back on for us."

I'm not alone here. Sid and I come together. Now, he's sitting a few feet from me, not reading, just looking out over the stream. He knows that I don't want to talk when I'm writing. He respects that.

So for an hour or two, I sit by the open doors, overlooking the stream. As I write this, the water shimmers. This is my quiet time. My time to listen, and to think whatever I wish, uninfluenced by momentary interactions with other people.

The sun is dropping in the sky. It no longer sends its direct rays into the cabin, but it highlights the pale green leaves at the swaying tops of the tallest sweetgums. It's now about eight o'clock, and in another hour the world will darken. Will it be too cool for the whippoorwill to sing? Is July too early for cicada songs? I'll wait and listen.

July 20, 1996

Sensory Richness

This is the first summer night we will sleep over at our cabin this year. Sid has cautioned against it because he didn't want us to get Lyme disease on top of my recuperating from pneumonia. Being here as day ends, and anticipating the beginning of tomorrow here, feels right. Staying overnight will be special: to hear the whippoorwill, to sleep in the comfy feather bed, and to look out the window as the light dims . . . . .

In the early dawn, I can see pine trees, the sky, and hear morning sounds mingled with rustling leaves. The cabin is still and quiet.

During the day I'll want some quiet time in lieu of the classical music that Sid enjoys. Not only can I hear the wind, the leaves brushing against each other, I can smell the fresh stream water. It's as if one sense facilitates another sense—or thwarts it.

July 21, 2001

Cabin vs Paris

I've thought today that being at the cabin is preferable to being in Paris.

We spent almost a week in Paris last month. I had enjoyed it. I was not sorry to leave.

Reviewing my time at the cabin over the past few decades, here is where many meanings of my life have been centered. This place has to do with me and with Sid. At the cabin, somehow I'm more open to new ideas and experiences: reading a new book and feeling part of the natural world, than when I'm in Paris.

Butterfly weed

July 27, 1985

Connected Worlds

After a brief shower, the air is moist. The leaves are motionless except when a drop falls from above (either onto the leaf itself or onto one nearby). Then there is a quiver, until the motion stops a few seconds later, and all is still again.

A breeze now catches the branches up high in the sweet gum. The post oak's larvae-eaten leaves are fifteen feet above me. They tremble. Down here by the cabin only the individual water droplets make the leaves quiver.

Looking more closely, I see the small sweet gum is touched by the moving air. This is the tree I trim each spring, to keep it no more than six feet tall—so that it won't obstruct the stream view or grow tall, over the cabin. Its top is level with my head as I sit here by the big screened window. The tree's movement is slight, and the four or five droplets on the stems of the upper leaves seem stationary. They remain equally spaced. When a droplet falls onto a terminal leaf it does not disturb the drops on the leaf's stem.

Throughout the morning, the sky has been overcast, but now vague segments of blue appear—and golden rays of sun alight on the mountain laurel. The pale stems of this year's leaves suddenly are lemony, and the seeds from this year's bloom a vibrant chartreuse. As I write, the sun disappears, the patch of sky blue is veiled in cloud, and the tapestry of dark branches and green leaves stands quiet in front of the grassy bank and brown glistening stream below.

Above today's cloud cover, is the drone of an airplane engine. If I don't listen carefully, it's gone, but when I pay attention the sound lingers. The military base nearby is probably the source, carrying a muted threat of violence and war. There is no peace and solitude to be had for long in this world. As I hear still another plane nearby, the pulsating call of the flicker intrudes. The bird calls me back to hear the wren's chirp, the stream's ripple, the drip from the roof. The wren, little larger than a brown laurel leaf, moves from branch to branch—silently.

Again, the droning of a heavy-engined plane.

How do these two worlds connect? Is the wren's world completely separate from that of the plane and its pilot? The earth beneath them is the same. They fly through the same air.

 I can more easily imagine the end of all airplanes than the end of all birds.

July 29, 1989

In the Dark on a Summer Night

In the daylight it would never occur to me to want company walking nearby trails. What is it about the dark? I feel anxious being alone outside after dark. Something about the dark intrinsically alarms me. I can't see very far away, and I've learned that darkness can cover threat. Is that a cultural belief or idiosyncratic to my upbringing?

Reminds me of the cartoon that's long been on the door of our gas refrigerator:

Panel #1 shows a man holding his worried little girl, with his young son holding on as well.

Daughter: "Are there any really dangerous creatures out here in the pine barrens daddy?"

Father: "Yes."

Son: "What kind?"

Panel #2: Father, looking at broken whiskey bottles, burning camp fire, tire floating in stream, graffiti on tree, hunter in background: "Humans."

Last evening as we returned from a stroll on our sand lane, whippoorwills called in the distance. Suddenly, near the entrance to the garden trail we heard a watery "BLP." We stood still to watch a heavy-bodied whippoorwill fly between pine trees just close-by.

When we were back in the cabin, the inside was completely dark, and I lit a kerosene lamp to have it reflect the welcoming comfort of walls, rugs, and chairs.

Some nights, I'll take a flashlight and walk alone to the outhouse. Just now, in the dark, I comfortably walked alone, and I had no fear. I felt a reaffirmation that the world here is full of natural wonders such as whippoorwills and long dark nights. Other nights, Sid will sense my reticence and walk out the path with me, and I've had the impulse to tell him to return to the cabin without me; but I was comfortable that he was standing a few yards away.

Does darkness hide a potentially hostile world? What is it that I fear? For over two decades in the pine barrens, we've spent days and dark nights in a cabin on this stream. I never felt any personal threat here from other humans. Maybe my protection against unseen evil others is my strong companion, Sid. I primarily see him as reassurance that my world is benign . . . .

Thinking about the darkness of night, I continue to feel both protected and anxious, both comfortable and insecure, both strong and vulnerable.

Clethra in bloom

Clethra past bloom

August 2, 1985

Looking at a Bird

Late this afternoon a small bird was peeping, as it sat on the porch railing. I stood at the door watching it for a minute or two, while it looked at me. I noted its yellow washed, slightly spotted breast, its wing bars, vague eye ring, small narrow beak: a pine warbler? And then I had a sense of completion. I now had identified it as best I could.

The bird could be categorized. It was a warbler. It seemed to be an immature bird, and maybe that's all I could see. But it was an individual, a unique one, and rarely when I look at a wild animal do I think of an individual. I'm likely to name, categorize, and then go on, look elsewhere as if I had really *seen* the animal.

Maybe I can look more closely from now on, at the way the tail is held, how the animal responds to a puff of breeze. Maybe I can look more at the individual's uniqueness, look again, and again.

August 3, 1996

My Favorite Place

There's a comfortable rhythm here at the cabin. This is my favorite place. Until I wrote that, I never thought of the cabin in that way. I have often said that if I had to choose between vacations to far off places and time at the cabin, my choice would be clear: no more distant places. But that is not saying that the cabin is my favorite. Is it because I can hear the *brr* of the hummingbird's wings here? And watch her perch on the dead sassafras tree to let the sweet water drip down into her tiny body? Is it because Sid and I are together and alone here, each sharing our own and the other's enjoyment of this place? Because life here is simple—few unimportant things. Enough water and food brought in, comfortable bed and chairs, easy to clean and maintain.

There are events, intrusions here that we don't control: wild animals in the house, trees fallen in the stream blocking our canoe; heat, cold, rain—these are part of the area and feel "right." That's not the case when a stranger comes in to steal our canoe, our tools, down sleeping bag. And the ticks live here—pesty, ubiquitous, many carrying Lyme's disease. We wear our various uniforms of white that symbolize our recognition that ticks are here, and we must accept them, though we attempt to minimize their bites and to escape the disease they carry. The ticks in a way enable us to proclaim how special this place is for us. After all, we persist in being here in spite of the ticks. They help us affirm the depth of our love of the cabin. This is not the garden of Eden; it *is* part of our lives.

August 10, 1996

Living with the Past

Here I am, 67 years old. From my earliest days I often heard people remark about *new* and *different* things. The value of something seemed much greater if it were new, different. Surely, women's clothes, emphasize novelty. Admire a dress of a friend and she may dismiss the compliment with "Oh, it's an old dress. I've had it for years." Things we use or enjoy—appliances, cars, furniture, even art work—are prized by many others if they are different, new. Travel is often reflective of this theme, rather than "going back" to the same place again, there is often a tug to plan a vacation where we've never been.

As I look around me, my comfort and pleasure often come from the old, the expected, the same. In relationships, I treasure my husband, children, old friends. I welcome the familiar surroundings in our home and in our cabin. I enjoy wearing old clothes.

The joy of the old and the familiar is the comfort in being in a known and predictable place—psychologically, socially and physically. Beyond that is the excitement and joy in subtle changes, nuances noted for the first time. The old forming the ground on which the new stands.

Seeing Cezanne's pine trees was the highlight for me of a recent museum exhibition. I felt he *knew* pine trees, and interpreted/painted them to communicate his knowledge and feelings about those trees.

When we walked the familiar lanes of Whitesbog this morning, I gasped on discovering a patch of foxtail lycopodia, and across from it, a solitary bloom of fringed white orchis. Toward the end of our walk, we watched a large indigo snake sunning itself along the roadside, and then saw it slip into the clethra. These are new and different events, occurring in an old place. When we return to that path our walk will be enriched by the plants and animal we saw today.

When a new experience occurs, it is especially pleasurable and meaningful if I can relate it to the past and can draw on it in the future.

Oak leaves eaten

August 11, 1984

What Draws My Attention Today

The telephone and the doorbell never interrupt me (we have neither), but I have frequent, unexpected occurrences that I see and hear:

As light begins in the eastern sky, I listen to the whippoorwills. It seems there is less urgency to their morning songs, but of course it's the end of their day.

I heard the jet black headed male towhee jumping in the leaves below our screened stream front. Then suddenly he flew up into the post oak to call "ku-ree." He has flown from branch to branch for the last few minutes, calling out to his mate?

The red squirrel has a compelling bubbly chatter. When we first spent time down here, we thought he was a noisy, elusive neighbor, but now we hear his familiar voice as a natural part of our rarely quiet world.

Mid-day, the tiny calls of young chickadees herald the frequent gathering of young birds near the cabin. The "neeping" of the nuthatch creeping up the pine tree trunk; the immature pine warbler flitting from one pine branch to another; the orange flank of the titmouse catching the sunlight as it flies about; and high up toward the very top of a sweet gum tree is the male scarlet tanager. It's hard to believe he's only seven inches long, because the vibrancy of his red head and back are so easy to see many yards away.

When the air is damp and heavy, the rustle of leaves says rain is on the way, and I await the droplets. The beginning raindrops of a summer shower or storm are welcome. The dull taps on the leaves is a cue. The rain often comes along with the breath of wind.

A bobwhite is calling from the west. Somehow the two main notes fly over and through the woods to me.

I enjoy the katydids on August evenings. A pulsing rhythm pervades the twilight air. Their chorus promises that the woods are alive and busy, at just the hour we begin to think of sleep.

August 12, 2000

Rainy August Afternoon

It's not a typical hot, sunny mid-August day. It's 4 p.m., and very dark. I can barely see what I'm writing.

Rain has started. I hope that it will help the horsemint Sid transplanted to thrive.

The usually smooth stream is pock-marked with rain drops, each crowding others out, with the resulting complex pattern of circles, little waves interrupted by larger waves.

In heavy rain, every leaf on a branch twitches and vibrates, never still.

In light rain, leaves are motionless until a drop of water shakes them.

The cedar boards on the deck are slippery with a coating of algae. There are a few puddles again along the edge of the screen porch. We're dry inside. The air is cooling; the dampness increasing. We'll have dinner in a few hours, and maybe it'll be inside instead of on the porch. Thunder is in the distance. Thin, parallel threads of water come off the roof. As the rain lets up a bit, the drips change to rows of long parallel beads.

The sound of rain has a special rhythm. Muted coins on the laurel leaves sit along the perimeter of the cabin.

Water-on-to-water as the stream moves by catching rain drops.

August 13, 1977

The Mantle Clock

The old wooden clock stands on the rough stone mantel over the fireplace. The clock's frame stands over a foot high, and its face is dark. One must look carefully to see the dulled hands point to the 12 shiny numbers. For us, it always announces the same time—10:25.

I turned the key twice, and the clock struck twelve. After winding it some more, I set it. And now the TICK, TICK, TICK pervades the room. At first, I looked at the clock pleased that after a few years we had started it working so easily. I didn't notice the tick, tick, when we were talking, busy eating, cleaning up, or when the rainstorm came by.

Now most all is quiet here, and the rhythmic sound is loud. I want to stop the pendulum, but first I wondered why?

It's an unnecessary intrusion. There's a wrist watch in the other room, and we each have a clock "built in," so that we know whether it's morning, or afternoon. We do not want to live by the clock down here. The noisy tick announces the continual passage of time.

I stopped the heavy pendulum in mid-swing, and let the quiet rush in.

It's after lunch, and I look up at the clock. I know it has the potential to burst into a regular ticking, striking clock. It's coiled and ready, only awaiting the touch of a hand on its pendulum.

The way I spend my time here is up to me. I need no reminders to control when I start or finish.

As we locked up the cottage for the week, I set its pendulum swinging. When we come back here it will have wound down to silence. The mantel clock will not be used again. Let it stay that way.

Early colors on maples

August 13, 1995

Watching and Waiting

Last night a few minutes after eight, it was growing darker, and we were reading by the light of the kerosene lamp. I went into our bedroom to see the flying squirrel's nest, and wait until he/she scrambled up the shutter and out into the night. The nest was just a darkish area tucked on the left end of the windowsill, between the window and the shutter. I sat watching and waiting. I assumed that I was not too late to see the squirrel leave, though I couldn't be sure.

Sitting quietly, watching and waiting was a pleasure, in part because I was the passive observer of a simple natural occurrence. Maybe the squirrel didn't know I was there. What the squirrel did wasn't dependent on me. Perhaps s/he was waiting until the sky became a particular hue; perhaps the intensity of katydid's song had to reach a certain level; perhaps the squirrel was still asleep, wakening later than she/he did in past nights.

All of a sudden, surprising me, though I had been awaiting it, the squirrel scrambled up the shutter, blurring the opening at the top—and then all was quiet. It was a special time—full of paying attention, waiting and watching.

I imagined how it would be, in a few weeks, going to see our expected first grandchild, waiting and watching, seeing the new baby as she enters this world.

Fern in woods

August 21, 1977

Sitting and Looking

We often walk along the woodland trails. We note stands of pine, oak, gum trees, and the fern and isolated flowers or shrubs.

We like to paddle on the stream, noting turtles as they slip into the water when they sense our approach. And we watch the damsel flies dart and laze on the pads of spatterdock in the backwaters.

But we see most, when we move least. A friend and I were watching birds in the woods of Maine one day. He said, if you stay in one place and sit and look, you'll see all the birds and animals in the area.

Before noon today, I sat near the stream. A rustle in the bush suggested a chipmunk or squirrel, but none appeared. A yellowthroat darted out of the clethra bush just three feet from me. She looked at me for ten seconds, her yellow bib vibrant, her feathers sleek. Then she flew to a blueberry bush, then the swamp maple, and across the stream into the clethra.

Moments later, the chipmunk appeared in his hole on the stream bank, looked around, and holding still for a bit, dashed into the bush, and was gone.

August 26, 1977

Boredom

I've been thinking. Now, at age 48, I look at my days at the cabin with never a moment of boredom. We have no TV, minimal radio, seldom read newspapers, rarely a visitor, no mail or phone. The time speeds by all too quickly.

What does it mean to say, "I am bored?" Basically it means that I am not satisfied with my current situation. That I would like to be away from this time and place. It is a denial of the value and desirability of the *now*.

People have often asked, "What do you '*do*' at the cabin? I'd be bored." You might be bored, but not me. This is my life and I love it!

August 26, 1988

A Spider

Yesterday afternoon I noticed a plump brown spider, just outside the screen porch. As I glanced away to see if a hummingbird was at the feeder, a movement outside the screen drew my attention back to the spider. It was making a web—going up and down, round and round. It worked quickly, stopping its rhythmic trail only briefly. It continued until dusk, and maybe after dark.

Today, at breakfast I noted that the spider was motionless, out in what looked like midair. I went outside to see it more closely. It was in frantic motion—entwining a fluttering fly in a web.

Now, a few hours later, I see one thin strand of web hanging from the porch roof, but no web, no spider, no fly. Again, I live with nature's mystery.

August 28, 2005

The Past

How do I blend the past and the present? So often I do the same things I've done for decades. When I sweep the screened porch in warm weather, I recall the annual spring pollen on the table, a dried salamander on the floor, the window pane we broke when the front door was stuck closed.

"Recall" implies that I try to remember, that I seek to think of the past. But the thoughts are *in* me, they are not called back. When I see the stream so low that both entry posts have feet in the mud, I also see water filling the banks way up to the nearest pine tree.

Here I am almost 76 years old. Do these thoughts of past and present emerge more and more because there is so much past, that it keeps tumbling out? Is one reason that I like the cabin and feel comfortable here, because past is all around me here? It cradles my days.

At the cabin, the pace of the day is slow, largely unplanned. This lets times past sit with me. There are few new things here. I can think of two: a hand cranked blender so we can make gazpacho, and a headlamp to help Sid when he washes dishes on increasingly dark nights.

Most everything in the cabin is many decades old. Some pieces are tied to people or places that have meaning to me: the rug underfoot, the round table with the embroidered cover under glass, the oil painting of cedar trees, the clay wall-hanging, my photos. Each is a part of this place, and a part of me.

In my old age, I drag, carry, hold on to the past, and memories flow into the present. When I'm gone, my memories will disappear. It's useless to make a list of these things for any next persons who live here. They would have no associations with people and times gone. Each thing is given life and meaning only by me or by Sid.

Blueberries over stream

August 30, 1985

Being Here

Sitting here—being here—little is asked of me beyond the daily activities of living: eating, housework, gardening. My mind can relax. I can sit, open eyed, listening—not searching, not puzzling. Just being.

A sleek, colorful male redstart just dashed into the sour gum tree. The red leaves of the tree look like a hundred perched red starts now, but I know the bird has already flown off across the stream.

As I sit and look, my eyes fall on a sun-soaked leaf, or a slim maple trunk leaning over the stream. I can be still—as the brown stream floats by. I can feel the breeze-neither warm nor cool.

I'm not doing much of anything . . . but in my own terms I am *being*. There's no purpose in this . . . no one will get anything from all this time I sit and *be*.

Someone might suggest that I am wasting time. This is a pleasurable experience, in the sense that I am not tense or searching. I am able to doze off a bit, look around, listen. This is no mystical experience. I can watch a red squirrel scurry across the lower branches of the sour gum. I am here, on this chair, I am me.

This is my time. Sid respects it—and though he comes across "interesting" items in his newspaper, he refrains from telling me about each one.

Sitting here enables me to feel that I am here; to feel away from home, work, and problems of the world. Have I built a cocoon here?

September 1, 1990

A Small Moth

In the kerosene lamp's circle of light, I saw a tiny brown thing. A small piece of twig? I put my finger on it, and when I drew it back I looked closely to see a small moth quiver, its wings folded. Again, I put my finger on it, and brushed it a few inches away. Now it is motionless next to my yellow pencil. What have I done? I move it closer once again, and I see little movement. My flashlight's beam shows the moth upside down, its slender body is moving side-to-side. I took it carefully outside, with little hope that it can survive.

What have I done? Must I intrude into the life of such a creature? At first look it reminded me of the small moths that periodically infest our house. There we squash a moth with impunity. It leaves larvae to eat our cereals and grains, others make holes in our woolens.

If the moth were a spider or a wasp, I'd carefully slide it into a cup and put it outside unharmed. But if it looks like a weevil, a troublesome moth, I'd just maim or destroy it.

I find no guilt in swatting a mosquito, before or after it bites me. Does might make it right? I truly have a sense of satisfaction, when each tick I find on my white clothes goes immediately into a jar of alcohol.

What insect is of no count? What is "right"? What is "wrong"?

September 1, 1990

Texture of Place

Being here at the cabin lets me experience this place in many ways, over many years, diverse seasons, times of day, weather.

I know the texture of this place in late summer. I hear the voices of katydids, never quite in unison, rhythmically together making the heartbeat of the evening. I feel the immediate touch of the water when I take a dip in the stream. I smell the pines.

When I leave these woods and travel to a distant place, I experience only a shallow sense of what is there. This summer's trip to the Norwegian fjords brings memories of undifferentiated views and brief experiences, tumbling onto each other. Can I really *see* any place, *hear* any place, be fully *in* any place if I am there only a few days or a week?

The only place whose sensory texture I know is here, at the cabin, in these woods. I am always seeing it anew. Today a beam of sunlight touched grey lichen on the base of a familiar tree—a vibrant shimmering silver I had never seen. Today, I walked by the slender bud of a blazing star, a reminder that I've enjoyed it over years past and a promise that next week will bring its full bloom. The turns of the stream are always the same, but now when the water level is almost two feet higher, the stream's banks look strangely new.

I have a deep relationship with this place, its texture remains with me.

September 1, 1985

Aging

I washed my face this morning, and the light coming in the bathroom window made harsh shadows. My chin-line is not firm. My eyes are set above puffy lines. I look older. I look old. I told Sid that my face and his face are looking older. Sometimes, most of the time, when I look at him, I overlook details of his face. He looks the same as ever. Other times, that seem to occur more often, I look at him, and his face has deep lines.

My face looks like the person I am becoming, not the 56 year old person I am. This may be how I learn about, and accept my aging and the passing of time. My hair used to be chestnut brown, then a few lines of grey, and the brown persisted through the increasing grey. Now (I must go to the mirror first before I write) now I can still say my hair is brown . . . but it's more and more grey. I'm not ready to see that the grey predominates. Does it? When will it?

Yesterday I walked up to the picnic area and most of the bracken fern has lost its green, and turned a mottled brown. There is no uniformity in bracken. Some fronds are still fully green, a few are brilliant yellow and exceptionally beautiful among the green surround. Most fronds are already brown in segments, with sections where green persists, even with edges of bright yellow. And many are fully brown. It is their time. The fronds still stand tall. In some areas there are scores of these feathery brown umbrellas six inches over the blueberry underbrush. The bracken growth has stopped this year, the leaves will later shrivel, and stems will fall. Next year new delicate pale green fern will push up, rolled tightly until it is their time to unfold into the warmer months.

I know this year's procession of the generations of fern. With my own inexorable aging, the rhythm is harder to know. I keep standing strong as the green bracken, knowing that I will wither and gradually turn brown in others' eyes.

September 2, 1989

Using Old Things

We have had our VW Rabbit over five years. When we bought it from our friends it was a stopgap purchase, to last us a year, maybe two. The rear fenders had notable rust spots that I thought would spread quickly, demanding expensive bodywork or a new car. Now the rust spots are not even double their original size. I joke that someday I'll start the engine and drive away, leaving the rusty body behind—but that is decades away.

Almost ten years ago, old Sam Cowell, who lived nearby, painted the small wooden floor in our screened porch. He also painted the outside deck, but that decayed within a few years and has long been rebuilt. The screen porch is still solid, just two of the floor boards are a bit weaker. I had expected that those boards would snap, needing replacement. Someday probably, but they're fine for now.

Every meal we use the brown and white dishes that sit on the kitchen shelf. They look like new, although they were gifts when we were married 35 years ago. The grey towels we take down to the stream when we swim are the same vintage—wedding gifts.

As I look around the cabin, I imagine it must appear very much as it did when it was built, well over fifty years ago. The same wooden floors, the windows, the mantelpiece, the pump handle, the small wood stove. In our ten years here, little has changed, and I'm content to keep it as it is.

September 4, 1993

Red Squirrel's Nest

Over three weekends, we watched the red squirrel's nest.

First week, it appeared as a shoe-box sized mass of shredded bark and thin grasses between the bedroom window and the old wooden shutter. Second week, there were quivering tiny pale legs and tails so intertwined with one another that we couldn't tell how many young were there. The mother came in and out, nursing, covering and uncovering her babies whose eyes had not yet opened to the world. Third week, the little ones had downy hair, were much larger. Their eyes were still closed. Two sat at the edge of the window sill, two others in the nest.

And now a week later, the space between the window and the shutter is empty. The squirrel family has gone, leaving us our memories. How naïve of us to think we could look through the window and squirrels would still be there.

September 4, 2004

Sour Gum Leaves Are Turning

There are many red leaves on the sour gum tree on the stream side of the cabin. Though the top third of the tree is still mostly green, the lower branches toward the south, and those reaching over the stream, are all turned either fully scarlet or with some lingering green at the leaf base—others are basically green yet mottled with irregular red dots. The dots are over each of the leaves, both the green ones—which to the casual glance appear green, and the red ones which blaze in the sun.

The leaden dark branches with their black twisted twigs are a striking ground for the vibrant leaves. It's not the upper green section that captures my attention, or the lower branches with each leaf a vibrant crimson, but the middle section where the mottling is pervasive—both in the single leaf and in the patterns among the leaves.

Through the branches, across the stream, are the cool greens of the cedar, and swamp maples. It is almost as if the sour gum were ahead of the rest, or more sensitive to the changing seasons—a sentinel of days to come for all the trees. The small green fruit are sparse, perhaps the flock of catbirds yesterday finished eating most which were left.

A shriveled, small maroon leaf just floated onto my lap. It's full of holes and its edges are dark.

A monarch butterfly lazily flew by a while ago. Now a swallowtail zigzagged through the branches. Cicadas are buzzing, and periodically a persistent gawking of crows drowns out all other sounds as three or four sit atop the pitch pines down the lane and make their presence known.

The contrast between the red and green leaves on the mid-branches, allows each color to be seen against the ground of the other—though it is the crimson that at first catches the eye. But soon I find that it is the *pattern* of the two, not one or the other, that I particularly notice.

September 7, 2001

Getting Dark

It's 8:20 p.m. The black outlines of the post oak and the sour gum trees are gradually blending into the deep grey sky. One star is high up in the oak.

I'm sitting a few feet from the screen doors. The only light in the cabin, except the little flashlight on my journal, is the kerosene lamp on the dining table.

Katydids rhythmically call and seem to answer each other. Crickets, and other unknowns buzz and trill, and the night air pulses. Sid is dozing in the chair, his breathing merges with the insect chorus.

The coolness of the evening air has fallen. Soon I'll slide into bed, under the smooth white sheets and the quilt. With the onset of night, I await the whippoorwill's call. Now the flashlight has dimmed . . .

I like the darkness here. It veils so many daily details of life. The world moves further away. Only when I have this pen in my hand do a few thoughts pour out.

Now, I'm sitting in the rocking chair.

My mind's at rest.

September 8, 1979

The Same Streambed

There was a hurricane in the Caribbean which came up north along the coast—and though its winds had dropped in velocity, it still brought a lot of rain to the area. The stream has risen up to the base of the pine tree now. It's more than a foot higher than last weekend. The water rushes by faster, and the familiar margins are below water level. It remains in the same streambed. The backwater just south of the cabin is quite full, the royal fern is not visible under the brown water. The outline of the backwater is quite predictable—and it promises to have a lower water level in a few days.

In a few places the stream has run into new channels—forming routes to shorten its zigzag course. These paths are shallow though, and have little likelihood of persisting beyond the week. The course of the stream is quite the same this year as last, and promises to continue for decades more, much the same as it has flowed in the past.

There is a flow to each of our lives—a pattern and design we tend to follow. We lay quite firmly in our own streambed. The ebb and flow of time changes us somewhat, but our temperament, our "way" persists.

When we have more or less opportunity, family, friends, we may shift somewhat— now moving at double speed, now lazing in a backwater. But our direction, our inner flow tends to move on in our streambed.

There are many different events that impinge on us—we have a daily cycle, a seasonal shift, and each external shift influences us. Instead of seeking a new channel and alternate routes, we might best get more in tune with our streambed— where we've been and where we are and where we may be going.

Sid among flowers

September 9, 1989

Change and Constancy

I feel a timelessness here at the cabin. Todays are much like yesterdays and tomorrows promise to be similar. For years, in early September, we have heard the crickets and katydids chorus, the whippoorwill at eventide, the unexpected fall of sassafras leaves.

The rhythm of the woods is part of the fabric of my life here. When something different appears it's an event to remember. This morning as we cut trail, we heard the bobwhite calling. We came back to the cabin carrying scores of chiggers, and with tweezers we tried to remove each speck of crawling life. Some chiggers move quickly enough for us to see their motion, others appear only as a solid dot until our hand lens shows their crab-like profile.

Just now I saw a dozen light green balls on a shrub—acorns growing for the first time on a young chestnut oak. Next summer they will appear again.

Why do I get pleasure in these recurrent events in the woods? I am both interested in the novel, as well as the common and expected. Once I see something, I enjoy the familiarity of its recurrence. I look at the nearby sumac bush, whose older, larger leaves have turned red first, the midsized leaves are mottled red and green, and the small terminal leaves are all green now. That is the same pattern of leaf coloring I noted in sassafras several years ago.

Am I saying that I try to make order out of what I see? to get an idea of the rules by which these leaves turn color, the oak matures with acorns, the chiggers arrive? I think so. These woods are complex, a seeming jumble of trees, of plants, of animals. Some permanence here; in microcosm amazing change.

Old trees topple and young ones compete to take their place. Yesterday, as we walked down the sand lane, a fence lizard scurried up the trunk of a big pine. In past years, but no longer, a larger lizard often settled on the far wall of the woodshed.

I can remember a few purple liatris blossoming near our doorstep. Now, in their place sweet fern shrubs stand four feet high. Nearby, in the past, a dozen horse mints flowered, now only two horsemints bloom. Even our actions here lead to changes: the small laurels that we dug from the center of a neighbor's lane have settled into our place and they give us spring blossoms.

Constancy is the dominant mode here, in spite of the cycle of the seasons and the subtle daily changes. The woods stay the same. Perhaps the stability here promises me a stability, a continuing good health, and a sense of timelessness within myself. For more than a decade, the woods and my own self have stayed much the same, some growing, aging, changing.

AUTUMN

Cabin in autumn

September 19, 1986

The Dark

It was dusk. Sid and I walked out our pale sandy lane. Katydids were buzzing rhythmically and their chorus was everywhere. My field of vision was limited as dusk led to darkness. I felt fearful and uneasy, and so we turned back. It was black outside, when I got to the cabin.

The familiar trail to the outhouse looks different at night. This compounds my unease. Shadows—thrown by a flashlight's beam—distort the familiar daytime perspective. Usually, I brave it at night and walk alone to the outhouse. Sometimes I ask Sid to walk the path with me. When the outside is dark, it closes in, comes right up to the front door with its mysteries.

I'm 57 years old, and though I have vague memories of childhood discomfort of the dark, I can recall no particular events that led me to have fears at night.

A few years ago, when we were sound asleep, a thick blanket of smoke crept in the cabin windows. We fled around 3 a.m. with wet towels over our faces, not knowing how close or dangerous a fire might be. As we drove down the lane toward Esther's cottage, all was clear and quiet there. Next day we learned that the weather, an inversion, had brought fumes from a small brush fire over a mile away. I've thought little about a possible recurrence of that scare, although fire at any time in these pine woods is a hazard.

Maybe I'm uneasy because I know that I have little way of seeing and being aware of what's happening out there in the dark. There's a huge world that I know nothing about. At night that world comes almost to my skin.

September 24, 1979

Life Around Me

I'm sitting outside, looking and listening. It's impossible to ignore the reds and greens of leaves against the inky stream water, and the blue sky with puffs of white cloud. The wind is blowing now. Most of the leaves hold tight to their branches. Some leaves sail horizontally as if they have a special place to go. One arcs gracefully down to my feet. The movement of the leaves as they swish and slide on each other is rhythmic—moving with the wind to a crescendo, and dropping off into a hush.

A yellow jacket is moving from one scrub oak leaf to another—while a second yellow jacket crawls over a pair of pea-sized galls below. When the first yellow jacket lands only an inch from the galls, the other raises its head and front legs (fiercely?) and the intruder flies off.

The sour gum trees, full of fruit, are in their blaze of color. Their lower branches are covered with scarlet leaves. Their upper branches are quite green as a whole, though half the leaves are dark spotted and a few are brilliant red.

The sassafras are special! Just as the leaf shape varies from smooth oval. To one thumb, to two thumbs, their colors vary from yellowy green to pale orange, to bright orange, and even brown.

Again a dragonfly sunning itself on the deck railing—with brown head and mid-body, and reddish hind body. Wings transparent, netted with delicate veins, and a spot on the front of each wing.

Few birds around—a phoebe perches near the cabin. Blue jays, more quietly than in warmer months, streak through the treetops. There's a persistent chirping now downstream—a red squirrel scolding? The underlying chorus persists—cicadas.

Leaves after rain

September 25, 1998

Living Here

My life here at the cabin is part time, a day or two a week all through the year. Sid and I come to this remote place and live simply. Here kerosene lamps and carrying buckets of water are part of our lives.

The inside of the cabin is not separate from the outside. Here we open up to the woods in many ways: to get water from the stream, logs for the wood stove, music of insect songs.

We bring in three to four gallons of water from home, and that's more than enough for cooking and drinking. Stream water, heated up on the gas stove, is fine for dishwashing.

Several years ago, I got up from the table, at night, and leaving the circle of lantern light, tripped over a footstool and went sprawling to the floor. No problem. But it could have been. So, we explored the possibility of getting electricity. We learned that we would have to make a twenty-foot swath on either side of the lane to let equipment in. That's totally unacceptable.

Here, one tank of propane is more than enough to run our stove and our refrigerator for years.

Being at the cabin is part of my life. It allows me to think and feel in ways I would not at home. It's a base of simplicity, away from complexity. It puts our home and work life into perspective. No mail, no incoming phone calls. Three years ago, we bought a cell phone, and since then we have had less than a handful of calls.

Newspapers are brought in, a battery-run radio is here, but these receive our attention in our own time . . . or not at all.

It may be that in some ways we are in control here, with few intrusions from work or social obligations. Where we are not in control is in the weather, the length of daylight, and the animals and plants that live here. We welcome the intrusions of the natural world.

We know that we do have an impact on the woods. We often cut branches from our fire trails, and along the stream when we canoe. Just now, a delicate moth flew to the kerosene lantern, vainly trying to reach light in the glass chimney. But the heat and the moth's frantic energy were too much for the small creature. It struggles no more as it falls to the oak table top—dead.

Fern

October 4th, 1985

Being at the Cabin

As we drove down Magnolia-New Lisbon Road on our way to the cabin, the colors of fall were clinging to the vegetation on the roadside—and I felt welcomed. A kind of ease and quiet crept into the air I breathed—and now back in the cabin, with a small fire snapping in the hearth, Sid napping in the chair, everything is still and calm. There's no need to move, or talk—or think. Eyelids droop and the pen pauses . . .

Looking toward the stream I see the dark water—an occasional leaf sliding downstream. Just beyond my arm's reach is the young sweetgum tree that I trim each spring to keep it small. The red mottled gum leaves are muted next to the brilliant red Virginia creeper climbing up the old post oak.

I am happy here. My casual glance always lets my attention come to focus on something new, different as well as familiar. When I "see" the small gum tree, I not only remember yearly decisions on where to clip its new growth, but also I see the earliest, then later swelling buds of its leaves—the terminal branch that died last year.

And the wood burning stove is familiar to each of my senses. We've dragged in a lot of oaks, casualties of the 1985 gypsy moth infestation, and we've saved large pieces for firewood.

The pump water has its own familiar smell.

Streamside colors

October 4, 1996

Leaf in the Canoe

A leaf has fallen into the canoe as we paddle upstream. The sun moves in and out behind the clouds. At each turn of the creek a new vista of now bright, now subdued colors await us. The full greens of some clethra stand in the shade next to the sun-touched pale green and bright yellow of other plants. The variety of colors and shapes are a pleasure to see—maples, oak, sweet gum, sour gum, Virginia creeper.

I catch sight of a maple leaf near my foot in the bow—reds, yellows, browns, some insect-bitten holes, a slender pink-orange stem. Patches of crimson, pale lemon, deep orange-yellow seem randomly placed, but the whole little leaf draws me to look at it again and again. Each time a new subtlety appears. When I turn it over, the colors pale, hinting what's on the leaf's bright side.

Only a couple inches long to its point, yet the vibrance in this one leaf is equal to the whole woods.

October 10, 1987

Time is Passing

Time is passing. The woods are moving further into fall. Many trees and shrubs are in full autumn hues.

I hear the cry of geese, and under the cloud cover see a huge wedge of birds, honking on their way south.

The woodshed nestles in a vibrant spectrum of colors.

The sumac is most all red, while the young maples still parade in green. Scrub oak leaves are losing their green to the yellows, bronze, and reds—only clinging to green around the mid-rib and main veins of leaves. The laurel has yellowed leaves on each branch. Sweet gums display new shades—their leaves are deep burgundy and the stems of each leaf are pale pink or yellow.

The sour gums are the first trees to have leafless branches.

It's another reminder of the passage of the seasons of my life as I approach my sixties.

Oak leaves

October 10, 1987

"Flow"

I'm sitting next to the screened doors, overlooking the brown stream. This journal is on my lap. In the background I can hear the Saturday opera. To me, the male and female voices are intrusive, distorted by the poor radio reception. I'm not enjoying the music. Sid, who knows the opera well, can appreciate the beauty of the melodies, as he transplants small laurel outside. To me it masks the tiny bird twitters, the brush of the leaves in the breeze—and intrudes on the quiet of this place.

Now, the roar of airplane engines come out of the north and disappear into the west. They are still in the faint background. Sid agrees to turn off the radio's music. The sun comes out, to heighten the colors.

Without the music, I can relax and the world is a more comfortable place.

I find that when I listen to music, my eyes see less of the woods. For me, music is not a background experience. When I listen, I withdraw my attention from other things. I stop observing the pines, thinking, writing. If I do two things at once, I cannot fully experience each one.

This brings to mind a concept of "flow," from the work of psychologist Csikszentmihalyi. During "flow," a person is totally absorbed in and concentrating on an activity—such as mountain climbing, surgery. I want to have many of my experiences take on this single, exclusive focus.

Opening to the next blank page, with pen in hand, I am concentrating and absorbed in my journal. Just now, I hear a faint noise and glance across the stream. Was it a bird's titter or wind in the leaves? Natural sounds from the woods are not an intrusion, they are part of my "flow." They allow the woods to come into my ken, and I welcome it. My journal and these pinewoods become one.

October 12, 2003

Returning to the Cabin

We returned from Australia ten days ago. A long time away: six weeks. It is as if we had stepped out of time. Spring was the season in Oz. Late summer and early autumn here had gone when we returned. It is a readjustment being at the cabin. The world here is the same, but it looks different.

I'm watching two titmice and several chickadees at the feeder, as they pick up a sunflower seed, fly to a nearby branch, hold the seed with their feet and open it deftly.

The clethra here has partially yellowed leaves now.

I'll never see or experience what I missed in these woods. Somehow returning to the cabin after being away many weeks makes me feel older.

October 18, 1987

The Tripping Stool . . .

Here I am sitting by the open door, overlooking the blaze of autumn color. Each year, Esther insists that the woods are on fire. The colors are vibrant yellows, oranges, reds and browns against the blue sky. The stream is no longer dark brown or black—it, too, reflects the colors in its muted way.

It's hard to think of anything but this blazing color. No breeze stirs the leaves, and for the moment each leaf clings to its branch. Now a reddish-brown sweet gum leaf drops down a few inches. It's perched in the crotch of the lower branch, with its yellowed stem askew.

There's an ache in my right arm, nagging and reminding me about last night's darkness rather than today's light. Sid had been sitting by the glowing fireplace. I had been reading a magazine extolling the pleasures of country living. As I walked into the living room, and away from the pool of light on the dining room table, I stumbled, tripped over the small wooden stool. I didn't see any hint of it in the darkness till my feet tangled in it, and I fell back, onto my right arm, my head gently resting next to the glass door toward the stream.

Such an unexpected fall. In less than one second, I was down on the floor, my unlit flashlight slipped out of my hand and slid across the floor, and I grabbed the offending stool, shoving it aside. Sid, startled, asked what I had done, and why had I been so careless in the dark.

There I was down on the floor. My arm felt uncomfortable and I was shaken (and shaking). Sid helped me up. He put cool wet cloths on my arm. I felt sorry for myself. Sid was very caring.

I took two aspirins, went to bed, and slept just fine—upset by the recognition that I had luckily (again) escaped any serious injury—and assured that life would go on much as it had been!

Now as I sit here, with the morning sun climbing in the sky, the ache in my arm is a welcome reminder, not of any mild stiffness, but of how well off I am. How good I feel. How good it is that catastrophe has been kept at bay once more. The demons of the dark, this time our wooden stool, have been unmasked, and in part their sting found to be comforting.

Lane to cabin

October 20, 1979

Friends Visit

This special place is fragile—it has its own quiet, its own pace—its own life—and it can so easily be shattered by people who are not in tune with its rhythm.

Last week, our suburban neighbors came for lunch, in a huge maroon Lincoln Continental, a drink of whiskey in hand, a pack of cigarettes. They left in two hours—but it's taken more than that to get rid of some of their image and their chatter, their intrusion. They have ideas of how we could change, improve, or whatever the place. They talked about things like TV, that seldom enter our thoughts here.

They backed up their car, barely missing our carefully planted St. Andrews cross next to a newly found lady slipper. Later, when we walked up the lane, we found a baby spotted turtle, crushed.

Now, our friend Pat is here with us. She's so in tune with nature and this place. She cherishes the weekend in early summer when she and her husband Bob were here with us. Two months later Bob died in an auto accident, and now—sitting on our porch—she's trying to make some order out of her world. She fits in here and is welcome. We share her pain and grief and hope the place can heal her wound a bit.

October 21, 1979

Sights and Sounds

It's 74° inside the cabin and now the thermometer outside is climbing toward 80°. A mild breeze periodically arouses the leaves from their stillness, only to have them tremble slightly, and then be motionless again. Now there's a stronger breeze—and leaves which have been secure up to now snap off from their twig home and float down.

Some of the yellow, brown and red flakes drop into the dark stream. In the swift running water they join the parade from upstream in the race around the curves.

A squirrel chatters near the north backwater. A chickadee calls toward the south. The yellow leaves and seed stalks of the clethra are outlined against the black stream; the sour gum has lost all its lower leaves, but up above the berries await the birds, and the orange leaves are securely set. Our eyes tend ever upward toward the brilliance of oak, sassafras and maple leaves against the cloudless blue sky. Down below, red teaberries are extra bright to catch our attention as they peek out below their round waxy green leaves.

Sand lane

October 25, 1985

Lying in the Hammock

Lying in the hammock.

It's a warm fall afternoon.

For the last hour or so I have just been resting—much of the time with my eyes closed, dozing, not moving my body—and only intermittently having thoughts or dreams. When I first lay down the sky was blue and cloudless. Once in a while a breeze rustles the remaining leaves high up at the treetops—and then a soft movement of warm air caresses me in the hammock. Now there are clouds overhead, with pale blue patches sliding by behind the cloud cover.

October 28, 1989

Leaving the Cabin . . .

I feel a strong tug to stay. There's a quiet here. I'm looking at the trees, their stillness, or their subtle shifting in a breeze. Also, I'm watching a brown one-inch grasshopper sunning on a blade of grass, and I'm examining the patterns of pale brown pine needles on a cushion of soft green moss.

The quiet I find is welcome in these changing and infinitely mysterious woods and stream. The blue sky has cottony clouds adrift. I can look and listen to the familiar, and the unknown, and feel closer to this little area.

Why do I want to stay?

In many ways, the changing seasons here demand my recognition of the passage of time. Is it possible that staying here delays the calendar a bit? Leaving, surely promises that things will have changed before I return. Staying lets me look more closely at what is here, leaving means I've lost this moment, and this stay at the cabin becomes a memory.

Leaving our suburban home brings up few of these feelings—that home, in spite of the gardens I tend there with real pleasure, represents stability. When we return we find it just as we left it. Here at the cabin, the woods have a heartbeat, a pace of its own.

Stream in color

October 29, 1994

Withered Leaves

I look at the dry and withered oak leaves. They are no longer catching sunlight and making food for their tree. They are, however, still connected to their tree, and some may last months, just as they are. Makes me think about old people living their last months or years, attached to their family tree—able to manage fewer and fewer aspects of their daily lives, rarely feeding others—holding on.

When the breeze makes the leaves flutter, the tiny stem holds. It was well crafted and maintains the tie. And even if the leaf should fall, there will be a permanent scar left, to remind me of the attachment that is physically no more. The legacies and memories are immortal, just as a leaf's components continue to build new soil and offer a foundation for new growth in coming springs.

Someday I'll be a withered leaf. I'll hold on fiercely 'til I let go.

Woods in back of cabin.

November 6, 1987

Themes of My Journal

Auden hailed Brodsky [Nobel prize for literature 1987] as a "poet of the first order" and a "traditionalist . . . interested in what lyric poets of all ages have been interested in." For Auden these included "encounters with nature," "reflections upon the human condition," and "death and the meaning of existence."

Clipping from New York Times *re Nobel Prize Laureate Brodsky*

These are the themes of this journal, not because I'd like to stretch to make them mine, but because these are my themes. I am not a poet, I write plainly, and I am of no order, certainly not of "the first order." These themes are those of all thinking persons, most everything else is commentary.

I write because I like to think, and the process of slowly putting my thoughts on paper allows me to consider life, reflect on my thoughts, and think again. When I sit down with this journal, pen in hand, I seldom have an idea that has driven me to it. I never lack for a topic.

Fern in woods

November 6, 1987

Cutting Trails

Glenn, our neighbor, brought his brush-cutting machine over to the cabin this morning. He used it on our trails. It's *noisy* (so we had to wear ear covers), it's *dangerous* (when chips of twigs fly off at high speed to my cheek, or an uncovered eye), and it's *fast* (it's whirring blade slices shrubs now mostly bare of leaves faster than the eye can see). Now, we have 50–75 yards of trails cleared in no more than an hour's easy work. All that's left to do is rake up the cuttings.

A question now, is it too noisy, too dangerous, and too fast? There is no pleasure, satisfaction in the noise—it's an engine's pollution, a price we pay on a temporary basis for the convenience. The danger—we must wear a mask and goggles, if we ever use it again. No harm to an eye can be a price we'd willingly pay.

Usually, when we cut trail we look at each stem, each branch and decide whether or not to cut it off to open up our way. If there's an ilex or a sweet fern, we'll skirt them—since they're relatively rare, and we enjoy seeing them thrive. The fast, sharp blade of the cutter allows no individual decisions, it clears everything in its way.

Some engines are fine in our lives—the car brings us here, and is an integral part of our daily activities—without it, we would forgo some things we consider "important." The brush cutter, on the other hand, is not going to be a part of our lives—we can find the world around us more easily without it.

We are not in a rush to cut trails—in fact, as we cut slowly this afternoon, we spotted a four-foot holly tree that we'd never noticed before. We trimmed the blueberries, smilax, and clethra around it, and now when we walk down that short spur to the prothonotary backwater, we can watch that holly as it grows.

November 9, 1990

Outhouse

A trip to the outhouse is a pleasure down here at the cabin. At home, or elsewhere, the few steps I take to a toilet have little or no significance in my life. They are quick transitions from one place or other to the bathroom, and back.

Here the short walk is special. Today, I leave the cabin with the wood stove on. The kerosene heater has cooled down after helping to move the thermometer from 40° to 66°. The air outside is still, no sun is shining. Pine needles and oak leaves cover the path. Each bundle of three slender needles has a dark end, and hundreds of the bundles of needles lay at crisscross angles to each other making a familiar pleasing pattern. The pale suede but veined undersides of leaves are tossed with the sleek, shiny darker tanned upper sides of other leaves. Firm paired red teaberries are along the path. I rarely pick and eat a berry here. I want to watch them as winter comes and they stand in a bed of snow. We walked down the lane and over to a neighbors' today, so we have had our ration of teaberries for now.

Terminal branches of the pines are scattered on the ground, evidence of the red squirrels' presence.

The outhouse is neat. I swept the leaves and cobwebs out earlier. But on each trip the little broom must be run around the toilet seat to discourage spider bites, and possible ticks.

The return to the cabin allows me to see the path from a new perspective—new teaberries, twigs for kindling, and more pine cuttings. It's quiet on the path today—only the distant chatter of a chickadee.

Once I'm back in the cabin, next to the toasty stove, I see the stream shimmer, striped with reflections of leafless trees. The red holly berries remind me that this cool day is the beginning of winter to come.

Fall leaves

November 12, 1978

A Warm November

A warm November so far—no killing frost yet. Only the oak trees hold on to their dry brown leaves. The blueberries have some vigorous crimson leaves attached.

The ground is brown with oak leaves, the sandy drive is blanketed, and in the walk to the out buildings, my feet toss papery leaves up and ahead. Few leaves are falling on this still afternoon. Occasionally, one parachutes down, and nestles with ones below.

A small breeze has arrived, and I watch a scrub oak leaf tremble fiercely, and then remain still.

November 26, 1998

Thanksgiving at the Cabin

This is the first time we've been here for Thanksgiving; the first time we've cooked a turkey in this hot (always 500 degree) oven. The impetus for us to be here, just the two of us, was the break in the routine of family Thanksgiving dinners. Given the choice of a welcome retreat to be alone in this special place, vis a vis blending in with a friend's family, we wanted to be here.

In some ways it's like being here on any weekend, but in other ways it's a very special time. As the sun falls below the trees across the stream, the cabin gets smoky from the roasting turkey. Sid sits with his book on Milton, his head leaning way to the right, his knit black and red wool cap askew—napping.

The windows are steaming up on the inside. When we arrived at mid-day, the windows were all coated with moisture on the outside.

This is a quiet, renewing time. I can just sit, look out at the dark stream, think about anything.

Family Thanksgivings have been a tradition all my life . . . but the family visit in two days seems quite as good. People have asked "Are your children coming in for Thanksgiving?" and I answer, "No, but they'll be here this weekend."

I can hear the loud ticking of the timer. When it finishes, the rice will be done. Time is moving on. In a few hours this Thanksgiving will be past. How many more will there be for me?

I have no image of an ideal Thanksgiving. This one is just fine, a special time for Sid and me, a turkey, a sunny afternoon for a walk down the lane, seeing familiar trees and bushes, quiet, in our place where we belong.

November 30, 2001

Quiet

Earlier today I turned on the radio briefly. After a short discussion of Mozart and Berlioz, and the latest news: economic intrigues around Enron's collapse, the war's progress in Afghanistan, and . . . and . . . I turned it off for the day. Too many "facts" or "news." I don't want to hear so much. I prefer quiet.

Now, Sid is sitting next to me at the table, we share the light from the two kerosene lamps. The windows and doors are closed. Tonight, the darkness outside is only partially pierced by the full moon. It's quiet here. The kettle was boiled for tea and is cooling down. I can hear my pen scratching on the paper. I can hear Sid turn the last pages of Proust's biography. The battery-driven clock is ticking.

This stillness is comforting. When Sid starts to tell me "Proust died of viral pneumonia," I interrupt and plead for quiet.

I think that when one sense, like hearing, is stimulated, then perhaps other senses might close down, or at least be less receptive. To appreciate the feel of our cabin and these woods, and to let me think about what I am writing, I can focus best in quiet.

When I listen to music carefully, I often close my eyes. What of smell? Of touch? If there is a competition between my senses, should I best focus on one sense?

Certainly, quiet helps me to feel and experience my world most deeply.

December 1, 2001

What We Don't See

Last night we left the plastic tablecloth on the porch table, and over the dark hours a breeze pushed the cloth onto the floor. This morning a crew of ants were scurrying all over it, amidst mouse droppings. We never see ants or mice on our screened porch. We also don't see the vole who visits the bird feeder at night time, and drops empty shells of sunflower seeds.

The woods here is alive with so many insects and animals—few that we see.

Sid chopping wood

WINTER

Cabin in winter

December 17, 1993

We Killed the Red Squirrel

Recent weeks we enter the cabin cautiously, looking to see what the red squirrel has done. The sofa cover is chewed and ragged, the Irish rug has curls of wool around it, a glass is toppled and broken, a canister is askew, the pillow on this upholstered chair has been chewed with remnants in the crevice of the seat. We have no idea where it enters, but it is a red squirrel. Maybe the same one we watched in the past, nursing its young as she rested on our windowsill.

It was pesty, inconvenient, to find evidence again that the squirrel was here. We worried that ticks may have been carried in. We wanted her to stay out, and had routinely put cotton rolls around the periphery of the cabin (for nesting material).

So we set a trap. A "have-a-heart trap." Left it set all week. The squirrel was dead in the trap when we arrived.

I feel ugly, two faced and sad.

Sid took the trap out the lane and buried the squirrel. Nearby, he found a large stand of trailing arbutus in an area due to be burned later this winter. Now, he's transplanted the arbutus nearer the cabin.

Meanwhile the squirrel is dead, we had no right to kill that little animal. She or he was living here, probably had more right to this place than we have. We're only here on weekends.

Earlier this year we set the trap, and a squirrel somehow turned it over several times, and got out before we returned! Imagine how frantic the animal was!

Now, I'd set the have-a-heart trap again, but only when we are here overnight. Then, we could know it was caught, and Sid could drive some miles away and release the squirrel to find another home. The alternative is just to live with the squirrel—and I'm not ready to do that.

I don't want to kill another red squirrel.

Lane from cabin

December 17, 2003

Sameness, Few Changes

We haven't been down here for several weeks. I missed the quiet, the woods, the sky, the outside-inside togetherness here. Much of being here is the cabin's sameness. It's just as it was last month, few changes.

Today, we cut back some branches that have fallen on the lane, swept the outhouse. I trimmed Sid's hair and left the cuttings on the ground. Maybe good for nesting material in the spring.

We brought the daily papers to the cabin. The news of the big distant world does follow us here. Hungry people going to soup kitchens are miles away. The battles in Iraq continue and are remote from us.

Trees' reflection on stream

December 20, 1998

Weekend at Cabin

Down here for overnight. The wood stove keeps us warm, with some assist from the kerosene stove. We will have a tasty lunch, dinner, breakfast and next lunch, before we leave for home.

We've done the usual things: walked over to see our neighbor Chris, to lighten her days (she's locked into a body that no longer allows her to talk, though she can understand everything, and can complete 1000 piece jigsaw puzzles). We walked some fire trail, and down the lane to the main road (noting small and large laurel that we've planted or just grew); swept out the outhouse (a shoe box full of pieces of pine cones chewed off by the squirrels in their quest for seeds); lighted the kerosene lamps at dusk (before 5); and we sat near their light as we ate and read a play (last night three acts of *The Winter's Tale*).

Morning drive to Whitesbog, where we walk around the reservoir, now low in water. We see over 50 swan calling, flying in smoothly and surely. We watch a northern harrier (marsh hawk), and great blue heron.

Now I'm back in the cabin, sitting in the rocking chair and writing, while Sid reads the Sunday paper about the impeachment of Clinton, and I'm ...

... watching the dark waters of the stream ripple by—reflecting patches of white sky, trees, brush.

... tending the wood stove as the flames die out, and feeling the temperature drop.

... pouring a second cup of jasmine tea from the teapot under the tea cozy.

... taking the flannel sheets off the featherbed, for a bi-monthly wash.

Now, I'm watching Sid transplant some pixie moss we dug up from the path at Whitesbog.

Lots of the day is spent in simple household tasks and eating. Nothing world-shaking, but the rhythm of our time provides a pleasurable comfort.

None of these activities are to be avoided. Rather they seem "right" and in a sense carry a morality.

The world outside may intrude when an army plane flies over a few times a day, or when the newspaper or radio brings news, but mostly there is a slow, even pace here. No long list of tasks to do, nothing seems "undone." Although, the curtains could be washed this year, and more cobwebs are growing under the table—things are as they should be.

Snow puffs on pine

December 24, 1993

In the Woods

This afternoon Sid and I walked some yards south of the cabin. To avoid the ticks, we hadn't been on that short trail for several years. Ahead of me, Sid used the long-handled clippers making a clean cut of sheep laurel, scrub oak and blueberry that had grown several feet tall. Shrubs have quickly claimed the trail. In warm weather, when plants are in full leaf it is hard to see a path. Now, my feet can follow the curves out to the tall holly.

I cut six holly branches, each with hard pointed leaves, golden and waxy, with their bunches of berries in threes, fours, and fives. We also passed a shoulder-high holly that we planted as a tiny seedling, and the balsam fir that a neighbor gave Esther almost a decade ago. Sometimes the only way we can follow an old trail is to watch for evidence of our cuttings in earlier years.

10 a.m. next morning—The feeder is full, and the birds have found it. Now, there is rarely a five-second lapse when the feeder is quiet. The tempo of their comings and goings is fast. Chickadees are most numerous and they share their perch with titmice and the red-breasted nuthatch. But when a white breasted nuthatch approaches, the smaller birds scatter. They often perch on the laurel that surrounds three sides of the feeder, or on the sweet gum that stands, stunted by my annual trimming, between the cabin and the feeder. None of these four species crack open and eat the seed while they perch on the feeder. Each flies off with a single seed to a branch, a trunk, or even cabin wall to peck it open.

December 28, 2007

Reading My Past Journal Entries

It's 6:30 p.m. The cabin is warmed by the wood stove. No need for the kerosene heater once the cabin reaches 60 degrees. I'm sitting in a pool of light under the kerosene lamp, with painted blue dogwood petals on its glass shade inches from my pen. Sid reading Saramago under the somewhat brighter lamp a foot away, with rows of painted pink roses climbing the side of his glass lamp shade.

I've just read almost all the entries to this journal—so full of my perceptions and thoughts. How little my thoughts have changed over more than three decades. How easily I can own words that I wrote many years ago.

Woods in snow

December 29, 2007

Woods on Fire

As we drove in the narrow sandy lane, we looked toward the sun. Orange-yellow dried bracken fern and dried leaves on the low scrub oak were ablaze. The woods seemed to be on fire! We had never seen that in all the years we've been here. The brown trunks of deciduous trees were in the background, and the slanty ray of the mid-day sun were back-lighting the fern and leaves. They shone orange.

There is so much to see here if we notice, and if we're here at the right time of year, month, day.

January 1 1993

I sit near the toasty wood stove watching the cold brown stream. Such a constant in my life is this stream. Its temperature varies, so does its depth, its speed—and the patterns of florets, blossoms, leaves that float down on it across the seasons. But in most ways it's the same. It curves in an "S" as it approaches and then brushes past the cabin. Right now its banks have expanded over the dock, almost into the near backwater, almost to the pine tree on the steps to our stream entry. What we call the "dock," is two upright posts, now well under water, just to the left of the steps that lead down into the leaves deposited by the eddies of the stream.

Time is like a spiral here—each year follows the patterns of seasons past—some a bit cooler or warmer, wetter or drier, longer or shorter, earlier or later. Spring always follows winter, and the same flowers bloom in sequence.

In some patches of our woods this year we have permitted "controlled burning." This will usher in new growth, snuff out others. Hopefully the deep accumulation of leaves and pine needles will have burned away, preventing the easy spread of small brush fires. This is our way of warding off a disastrous fire that could destroy the cabin and change our habitat in major ways.

There is for us in our personal lives as there is in our woods, a natural spiral of life. We accept and plan for its regularities. We balance continuity and change, each minute, each day of our lives. It is a challenge and a satisfaction that somehow we are able to be alive year after year with so much pleasure.

Ice in backwater

January 1, 1990

Throw Away

We are "away." We, like our neighbors in this society, throw many things "away," and though I am concerned about lack of landfill space, the perils of burning what we toss out, and the huge amount of waste we needlessly generate, I throw waste "away" many times a day.

What I toss into the trash is lots of mail I've never read, and irreparably useless items. Often these are the wrappings, or containers of food. Here we put the food scraps into our garbage pit, and dig the remnants into our garden each spring. We throw plastics "away."

Since I've been here today the trash includes:

> 8–10 paper towels (used to wipe up a cup of tea spilled on the floor)

> a paper container for 5 lbs. flour (that I put in a canister)

> several matches, used to light the wood stove, the kerosene lamps, the gas cook stove

> a couple dozen nails Sid pulled from some kindling

As we walked down the lane this afternoon we saw a bunch of white balloons, about 20 yards off. They had probably been released from a distant festive celebration, to go up in the air and "away." They landed here, so we have become "away."

January 5, 2008

Clock Stopped

When we arrived at mid-day today, I noticed that the clock had stopped. The second hand quivered repeatedly. It couldn't go beyond 2:46. I think I put a new battery in the clock last week when it had not been able to get beyond 4:29. So maybe the clock doesn't work anymore, or maybe it needs a stronger battery when the cabin gets pretty frozen at 19 degrees. I'll take it down and see if we can get it working again.

Meanwhile, there's no clock on the wall over the old wooden ice box. I now find myself looking at the blank space to check the time. I've looked there particularly after it got dark outside. Now, the cabin is only bright on the dining room table under the pools of light of the two kerosene lamps. There's a flickering glow from the wood stove, and periodically a flashlight helps us check the pots cooking dinner on the stove.

That clock gets a lot more attention than I realized. In a way it is easier to understand the meaning and value of something, now that it isn't here.

February 2, 2001

Changing Light in Sky

Sid and I spent an hour at Whitesbog, watching and listening to the swan in the changing light as the sun pierced the clouds. The sky floated on the open water, mirrored in pinks and yellows. No camera or painter could capture the changing light on this familiar landscape. The beauty was as ephemeral as life itself. Seeing it pass is not sad, or felt as a loss. I try to keep its image alive.

February 6, 1986

Weekend of Cold and Snow

The weatherman predicted snow, not to begin until late Friday night. We hoped to see the snow at the cabin, and the area covered in white. I remember the postcard we received from Esther several years ago, describing her joy in walking with her dog in early morning snow and her delirious thrill that the card shared with us.

So we drove down—arrived about 10 p.m.—to a cold cabin (32 degrees), a cold bed. A pervasive cold gnawed at our edges all night long......

This morning, the promised snow had come—covered the world, left puffs of white on pine trees, edges of white atop every branch. Gradually, we've warmed up the cabin—and now it's toasty......

What a joy! We see our familiar trails, the stream backwater in a never-before known WINTER. The snow transformed it all, yet it is all familiar. It's like seeing a beloved friend in a new way, something special that I'll carry in memory forever. The trunks of the pine trees with ridges of snow, the sheep laurel with white puffs nestled under last year's seeds, the quiet white of every trail, and the leaden segments of ice on backwaters and streamside. It's as if a new dimension of the reality of this place has been revealed. Come spring and summer, or the palette of autumn, I'll recall this snow, and feel that I know our woods better.

The trail to the woodshed has emerged, so clear and defined, though we used no shovel, only our footsteps set its outline. And over the day the path to the outhouse has gradually taken shape. Again, the outside here is personalized as is the cabin's inside......

Now, it's Saturday late afternoon. There is no barrier at the front door, even though it's warmer inside. The outside is part of the cabin: the paths, the trees and today's darkening sky. At the beginning of the long black hours, I feel a threat that all this coziness might seep out again tonight, and the cold outside could settle in.

I wondered, can a big log in the fireplace make any difference? The cracks around the doors, the uninsulated floor have begun to let the cold in. My knees are cool. A draft has let the line between "inside" and "outside" be blurred again.......

By sunrise I found that the cabin never got below 40 degrees. Under our quilts we had been comfortable all night.

1-6-80

Dear You Two:

Happy New Year!

I got your card from Porto Rico. Nice trip.

We had just 10 in. of snow on the picnic table! Temp. 15° above this a. m. Black water. White everywhere. Wish you could see it. No problem getting out.

Breaking trail tires the old lady. But its real great for a fun dog. He eats snow, rolls in it, blows in it, comes up with ice on his chest! Nice walk early this a. m. in beautiful full moon light. Indescribable! So I'm roving a little bit. See you again soon.

Esther

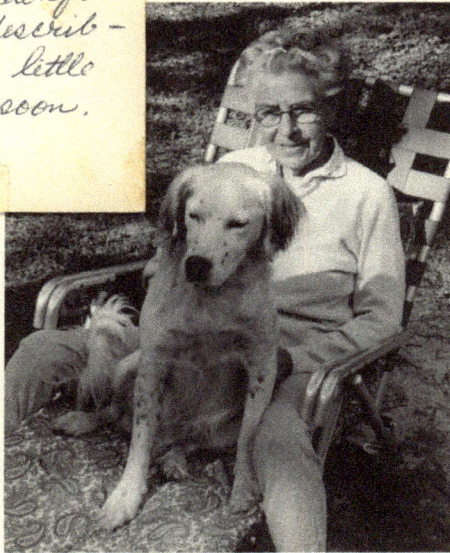

Our neighbor Esther

February 7, 1986

Thoughts from Esther

Esther and her dog, Pat, stopped by for a few minutes—to assure us she appreciates the things we brought her, and to thank us for our visits when we're down at the cabin.

She got to talking about hair, and revealed that last time she had her hair cut, she bought a wig.

It's something I have never had . . . and at my age I look forward to new experiences.

Then she explained that the wig would be very convenient for her, less time setting her hair, more freedom to get her hair wet in the stream—especially on hot summer days.

She is so dogged, tenacious in holding on to a full life—and sees her dog as therapy, as a goad to get out for early morning walks, and a demand to be active.

After she left, I looked at the postcard that she wrote us six years ago, now preserved under glass on our desk top. I specially saved it as treasure from Esther, now in her mid-eighties, who is so central to our life in the cabin. She wrote:

> *We had just 10 in. of snow on the picnic table! Temp is 15 above this a.m. Black water. White everywhere. Wish you could see it. No problem getting out.*
>
> *Breaking trail tires the old lady. But it's real great for a fun dog. He eats snow, rolls in it, blows in it, comes up with ice on his chest! Nice walk early this a.m. In beautiful moon light. Indescribable! So, I'm raving a little bit. See you again soon.*
>
> *Esther*

Esther Cope is a model for me that I'll continue to hold on to as I age.

Pine needles in ice

February 7, 1994

Day at Cabin

Monday. Took the day off from work to spend yesterday and today here. I had been missing time here in the rhythm of my days. I look out the double doors, over the bird feeder to watch the ripples and the reflections in the stream. The blue grey sky has dropped to the stream bottom and the browns of trunks and branches blur in wind-driven wavelets.

Sid is drinking Postum, and dozing in the chair.

One Carolina chickadee darts to the feeder, snatches a sunflower seed, and goes to his favorite perch on the mountain laurel where he hammers the seed with his tiny beak, eats the kernel inside, and then returns to the feeder.

A small, pale twig circles the curve of the stream as it moves in the brown water, through the blue of the sky, into the brown again.

February 8, 1992

Overnight Snow

Snow-quiet, soft, gentle. It paints new patterns on my world. It's slow—one tiny flake at a time. Although it's pulled to earth with the same gravity as rain or sleet, it gently sculpts each leaf and branchlet, each dry stalk of goldenrod, each blade of grass.

This is light snow. It may leave less than an inch of cover and disappear with a temperature rise. To be here at the cabin in this snow is a winter treat. Each week I hope the snow will come.

Although I catch my breath with the beauty of a first look outside in a morning after an overnight snow, I still prefer the gradual process of watching the first tiny flakes, seeing them fly—often horizontal—so light the earth hardly pulls them down. And then the question: will there be more snow to come, or is this a transient flurry?

Now, it's over an hour since the first white dust-like dots. This is real snow. How much longer will it continue?

The snow brings a different pattern to each tree or plant. The laurel leaves are flat and shiny, snow white settles at the petiole, where the leaf is connected to the branch, but the bottom half of the leaf is vertical and the snow slides right down. It nestles in the pitch pine needles where they meet at the branch. As more flakes fall, they cling to the slender needles.

When the snow began there was a greyness in the woods, as if the leaden sky dropped low. Now the woods are white, the sky turned white to match. In strong contrast are the almost-black tree trunks and branches, the vibrant green cedar and pine needles, and the tawny brown post oak leaves.

I want to go inside these snowy woods. We take a walk, down the lane, across the whitened black-top to the huge dead oak where birds sometime alight.

Now I realize that the snowflakes are becoming droplets. The patterns on trees and bushes are slowly melting.

Returning to the cabin, my view across the stream has changed. The woods are brown again, with zig-zag stripes of snow on a few branches. Most of the snow has melted off the leaves, and large white clumps are falling from branches.

Today for only a brief time the snow has turned the woods into a reverse of itself. Visually, it changed, and the quiet woods are no longer enveloped in white.

It is hard to hold on to the ephemeral beauty in a snowy squall in the woods. I hope it will stay in my memory.

Sid with canoe on streamside

February 19, 1994

February Snow

7 a.m., 60 degrees inside with the stoves going. We came down yesterday afternoon, drove the Toyota up the snow-covered lane. Dug snow away from the front door, and settled in. This morning, birds haven't yet found the seeds in the full feeder. Sid, wearing his red and black knit cap, is cuddled in bed under quilts.

Five or six inches of snow changes the woods. Every clethra, blueberry and sheep laurel is tucked under the snow blanket. The deep brown stream has grey patches of sky. The laurel leaves are still. Even the thin dried leaves of the post oak are motionless.

The sun has just painted golden bark on the sweetgums across the stream. Just the tops of the trees are in the light. Nothing moves in the cabin except the waves of hot air atop the kerosene heater. The only sounds are the subtle snaps of burning log in the wood stove, and occasional soft breaths from Sid.

The airplane engines have faded into silence. The titmouse calls from downstream. The sky is milky blue. My right foot is cool. I went back to bed with warm Sidney.

Later. Cabin in winter is much like cabin at other seasons. The furniture is the same, now we use the stove and featherbed for warmth. This time of year the windows and doors stay shut, so outside sounds are remote. Snow has drifted along the stream side of the cabin, and the water dripping from the roof has sliced through to the bare ground. In early hours, the shadows of trees and branches are dark on the white. Now at mid-day they're more subtle. Less stark in contrast to the gleaming snow.

The warm air today comes in soft gusts, feeling tropical.

The stream flows on—it is the symbol of life, moving gradually from upstream to downstream, from past to future. It stays here for only an instant, and like time represents the ultimate in continuity and transiency. As I watch it closely, I have a sense of sad acceptance. Sad because I know I can never sit here at this time again. There is a relentless current of life pushing me on.

> "But this—having been once, though only once, having been once on earth—can it ever be canceled?" Rilke

February 26, 1978

Place

The place I'm in certainly doesn't make me a different person. But the characteristics of the place do influence me, and can play a role in determining my mood, my activities and my attitudes toward myself.

The physical environment is difficult to separate from the social-cultural milieu. The brick-and-mortar aspects of surroundings is important. What's outside my window will play a large role in determining whether or not I look out of the window. When I'm here at the cabin, the outside has a strong pull. I look out the window, and I see ever-present stream, tufts of snow along the margins of the water, stark contrast of the white of the snow and the dark of the water as it smoothly flows downstream.

At home I seldom look out of the window, mostly to see if the sun is shining, if it is raining or snowing. Here, depending on where I sit, I am able to see the outside world, and check the activity at the bird feeder.

At home why do I rarely sit down and think by the fireplace? In part, because there are other things I think I should be doing. At home, there is no pull to look outside or to think about the complexity of the world.

At the cabin, it's comfortable and quiet to sit in front of the fireplace. The relaxation and easy pace allow as much sitting and being as I wish. Fewer things around make demands. Here, with a lot of inward drive I can follow onto whatever ends I wish. I can focus on my own thoughts of the natural world.

www.ingramcontent.com/pod-product-compliance
Lightning Source LLC
Chambersburg PA
CBHW061226270326
41928CB00024B/3342